CW01367657

ISBN: 9781313548625

Published by:
HardPress Publishing
8345 NW 66TH ST #2561
MIAMI FL 33166-2626

Email: info@hardpress.net
Web: http://www.hardpress.net

JC
359
C94

Cornell University Library

BOUGHT WITH THE INCOME
FROM THE
SAGE ENDOWMENT FUND
THE GIFT OF
Henry W. Sage
1891

# DATE DUE

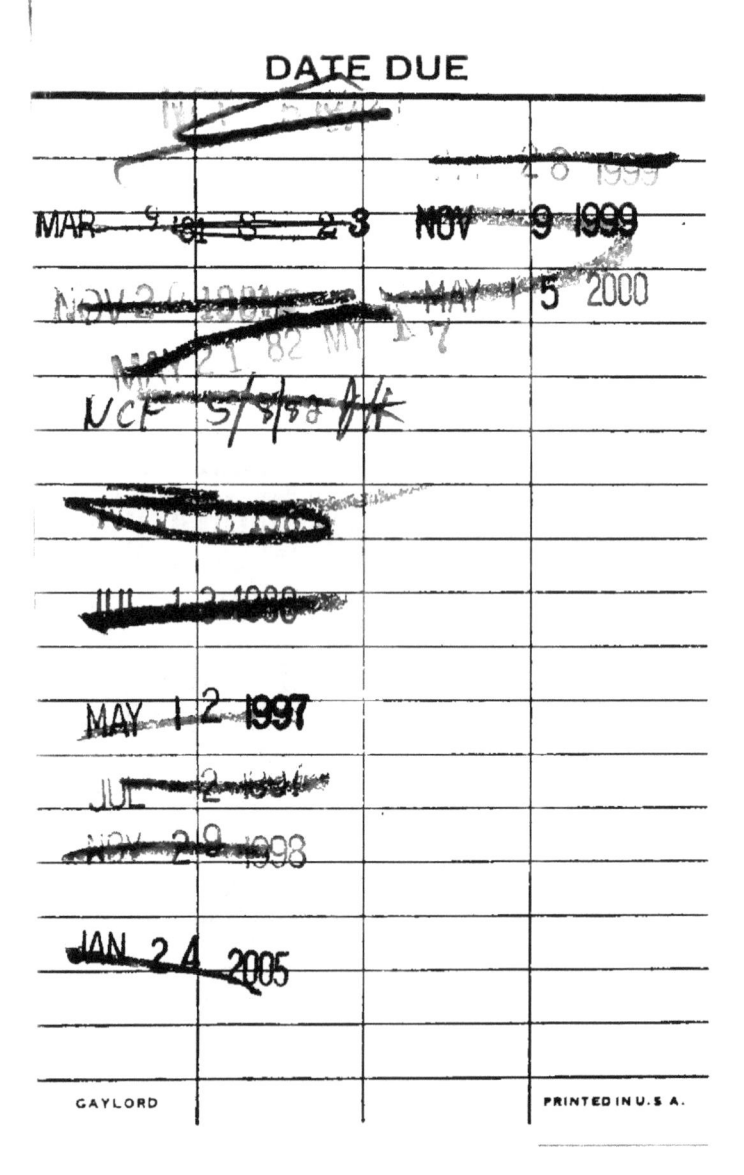

| | | | |
|---|---|---|---|
| | | | |
| MAR 9 '91 S 23 | | NOV 9 1999 | |
| NOV 24 1994 | | MAY 1 5 2000 | |
| NCF 5/8/98 | | | |
| | | | |
| JUL 1 2 1996 | | | |
| MAY 1 2 1997 | | | |
| JUL 2 1997 | | | |
| NOV 2 9 1998 | | | |
| JAN 2 4 2005 | | | |
| | | | |

GAYLORD      PRINTED IN U.S.A.

Cornell University Library
JC359 .C94

Ancient and modern imperialism,

3 1924 030 442 242

olin

# ANCIENT AND MODERN
IMPERIALISM

FIRST EDITION . *January, 1910.*
*Reprinted* . . *February, 1910.*
*Reprinted* . . . . *February, 1910.*

# ANCIENT AND MODERN IMPERIALISM

BY THE EARL OF CROMER
G.C.B., O.M., G.C.M.G., LL.D., ETC.

PUBLISHED BY PERMISSION OF THE
CLASSICAL ASSOCIATION

NEW YORK
LONGMANS, GREEN, & CO.
FOURTH AVENUE & 30TH STREET
1910

6/17/10

4.29+060

# PREFACE

THIS essay, in a very abridged form, was originally delivered as an address to the Classical Association, of which body I was President for the year 1909-10.

CROMER.

LONDON,
*December*, 1909.

ὁρᾷς, ἄβουλος ὡς κεκερτομημένη
τοῖς κερτομοῦσι γοργὸν ὡς ἀναβλέπει
σὴ πατρίς ; ἐν γὰρ τοῖς πόνοισιν αὔξεται.

"Dost see how thy country, when reproached for wanting in deliberation, looks sternly at those who assail her? For she grows great in the midst of toils."

Eur., *Supp.*, 321-323.

# ANCIENT AND MODERN IMPERIALISM

ABOUT the time when the Classical Association did me the honour of inviting me to be its President for the current year I happened to be reading a work written by a Hebrew scholar, in which I lit upon the following passage: "There is a saying of an old Hebrew sage: 'In a place where one is unknown one is permitted to say, I am a scholar.'"[1] I fear I am not sufficiently unknown in this country to permit of my making any such statement. I conceive, indeed, that the main reason why the presidency of the Association was conferred on me was that I might personally testify to the fact that one who can make no

[1] Schechter, "Studies in Judaism," p. 31.

pretension to scholarship, and who has been actively engaged all his life in political and administrative work, can appreciate the immense benefits which are to be derived from even a very imperfect acquaintance with classical literature.

Being debarred, therefore, from speaking to scholars as a scholar, I thought that I might perhaps be allowed to address the Association as a politician and an administrator. I determined, therefore, to say something on the analogies and contrasts presented by a comparison between ancient and modern systems of Imperialism. I could not, indeed, hope to say anything new in travelling along a road which has already been trod by many eminent politicians and scholars—amongst others, in recent times, by Sir John Seeley, Mr. Bryce, and Mr. William Arnold—but I may perhaps have succeeded in presenting in a new form some facts and arguments which are already well known. Plato, the Emperor Napoleon, and Mr. Cobden have, from different points of view, insisted on the value of repetition. Moreover, as an additional plea in justification of the choice of my subject, I think I may say that long acquaintance with the government and administration of a country which was at different times under the sway of the Macedonian and the Roman does to some extent bridge over the centuries, and tends to bring forcibly to the mind that, at all events in respect to certain incidents, the world has not so very much changed in 2,000 years. Whenever, for instance, I read that graphic account in the Acts of the Apostles[1] of how the Chief Captain, after he had scourged St. Paul, was afraid when his very intelligent subordinate whispered to him that his victim was a citizen of Rome, I think I see before me the anxious Governor of some Egyptian province in the pre-reforming days, who has found out that he has unwittingly flogged the subject of a foreign Power, and trembles at the impending wrath of his diplomatic or consular representative. When I read in Dr. Adolf Holm's monumental history that the Greeks in Alexandria, under the Ptolemaic rule, had the privilege of being beaten with a stick instead of a whip,[2] I am reminded that

[1] Acts xxii. 26.
[2] Holm, " History of Greece," vol. iv., p. 122.

to serve as a guide,[1] to form our own somewhat conjectural conclusions on this important point, This historical episode is, however, not without its moral in connection with the subject now under discussion. Dr. Holm contests the view advanced by other historians, notably by Curtius, that, after a meteor-like flash of supremacy, the Athenian character degenerated.[2] He does not admit the plea that the fall of Athens can be used as a charge against democratic institutions in general, but he points out that the kind of democracy which existed in Athens, notably after the death of

[1] Aristotle makes a very brief allusion to this subject in his account of the Constitution of Athens (c. 24), but he merely gives the number of knights, jurymen, etc., who were paid out of the contribution and taxes levied on the allies. One of the results of the extension of the Athenian Empire was to enlarge greatly the jurisdiction of the dikasteries, which, so far as I can judge, appear to have filled somewhat the same position as our Judicial Committee of the Privy Council. Grote, in spite of his manifest tendency to treat any defects in Athenian institutions with great tenderness, admits (Hist., vol. iv., p. 371) that the dikasteries were "not always impartial between the Athenian Commonwealth collectively and the subject-allies."

[2] Holm, "History of Greece," vol. iii., p. 195.

Pericles, was subversive of all good government; that, in the absence both of any executive government in the proper sense of the term, and of anything approaching to the modern system of party, the decisions of the Athenian people became merely a series of isolated measures, wanting in all consistency and continuity; and that not only broad political issues, but every detail of the administration, was submitted to the decision of the popular voice, with the result, *inter alia*, that a defective foreign policy was adopted, which brought about the ruin of the State.[1] If this view be correct, British Imperialists may derive some consolation from the reflection that the experience of Athens cannot be used as an argument to prove that democratic institutions must necessarily be incompatible with the execution of a sane Imperial policy, but rather as one to show the fatal effects pro-

[1] Lord Acton's verdict is equally decisive. In his address on "Freedom in Antiquity" ("History of Freedom," p. 12) he says: "The emancipated people of Athens became a tyrant . . . They ruined their city by attempting to conduct war by debate in the market-place. . . . They treated their dependencies with such injustice that they lost their maritime empire."

duced by democracy run mad.[1] The Athenian Commonwealth is, in fact, the only example the history of the world can show of an absolute democracy — that is to say, of a government in which power was exercised by the people directly, and not through the intermediary of their representatives. The fact that the experiment has never been repeated[2] is in itself an almost sufficient proof that the

[1] It has to be remembered that the Greek colonies were from the first independent. They were sometimes founded without the express authority of the Government, and without apparently any intention of increasing the power or enlarging the dominions of the mother-country. Sir George Lewis ("Government of Dependencies," p. 117) thought that "they were somewhat similar to the English colonies in America, especially after the independence of America." He adds (p. 179): "The non-interference of the Phœnician and Greek States with the government of their colonies did not arise from any enlightened views of policy, and still less from any respect for the rights or interests of a weak community. It must be attributed exclusively (as Heeren has remarked respecting the Phœnician colonies) to the inability of the mother-country to exercise a supremacy over a colony divided from it by a long tract of sea."

[2] Some analogy might, perhaps, be established between the principles advocated and—in so far, at all events, as Church government is concerned—put into practice by the Independents in Cromwell's time and their descendants, and those adopted by the Athenian Commonwealth.

system, in spite of the very intense and ennobling spirit of patriotism which it certainly engendered, was a complete failure.

Apart, however, from these considerations, it may be said that the conception of Imperialism, as we understand, and as the Romans, though with many notable differences, understood the term, was wholly foreign to the Greek mind.[1] The Greek language did

[1] I think that this statement is correct, but it is to be observed that pride of race, which usually accompanies the conception of an Imperial policy, was in no degree wanting amongst the Greeks. Thus, to quote one out of a host of illustrations which might be given, Euripides makes Iphigenia say :

βαρβάρων δ'"Ελληνας ἄρχειν εἰκὸς, ἀλλ' οὐ βαρβάρους,
μῆτερ, Ἑλλήνων · τὸ μὲν γὰρ δοῦλον, οἱ δ' ἐλεύθεροι.
(Iph. in Aul., 1400-01).

It will, of course, be borne in mind that in the days of Euripides the word *barbarian* merely meant non-Hellene. It was not till later that a different signification was attached to the expression (see Grote, Hist., vol. ii., pp. 162-63).

Grote (Hist., vol. iv., p. 389), speaking of the feelings entertained by Athenian citizens at the period when the hegemony of Athens was established, says that " among them the love of Athenian ascendancy was both passion and patriotism." The speeches recorded by Thucydides (i. 68-87) give a good idea of the fears and jealousies

not even contain any expression to convey the idea. A supreme effort was, indeed, made by one illustrious individual whom we should now call Greek to grasp at the dominion of the world, and thus turn the Greek mind in a direction contrary to the natural bent of its genius. But Alexander was a Macedonian, who would have been classed as a foreigner by the true Hellenes, and who ruled over a race possessing national characteristics differing in many essential particulars from those of the inhabitants of Attica or the Peloponnesus.[1] Moreover, Alexander was a conqueror

---

inspired by Athenian Imperialism, albeit its growth had but a few years previous to the delivery of those speeches been checked by a disastrous defeat, which necessitated the evacuation of Bœotia.

[1] Grote says (Hist., vol. ii., p. 158) that the native Macedonian tribes appear to have been an outlying section of the "powerful and barbarous Illyrians." See also vol. iii., chap. xxv., and Hogarth's "Philip and Alexander of Macedon," p. 4 *et seq.*

The right of the Macedonians to take part in the Pan-Hellenic contests at Olympia was at one time contested, but they were eventually admitted, as the Argive descent of their kings was considered to have been proved (Her., v. 221). Demosthenes said that Philip was not only no Greek, but not even "a barbarian of a place honourable to mention" (Phil., iii. 40).

rather than an empire-builder. He died before he could enter upon the constructive part of his career, and with his death the empire of which he had laid the military foundations dissolved. The most successful Imperialist amongst those who seized on the *disjecta membra* of his vast dominions was the first Ptolemy, and it is worthy of note that the principal reason of his success was that he did not attempt too much. He was not bitten with that lust for dominion which Tacitus described as inflaming the heart more than any other passion.[1] He was wise enough not to waste his strength in distant enterprises, but to consolidate his rule in Egypt and develop the commercial resources of the admirable geographical position which he had acquired.

Moreover, not only was the Imperial idea foreign to the Greek mind; the federal conception was equally strange. Although, under the pressure of some supreme necessity, such as the Persian invasion, a certain amount of unity of action amongst the independent

[1] "Cupido dominandi cunctis adfectibus flagrantior est" (Tacitus, Ann., xv. 53).

Greek States was temporarily secured,[1] it may be said that, at all events up to the time of the Macedonian conquest, the true conception of federation, which is a necessary precursor not only to the birth of national life, but still more to the successful execution of a broad Imperial policy, never took root in Greece. For the best part of a century prior to that date the history of Greece consists of a series of internecine struggles[2] and of tran-

---

[1] Mr. Tyrrell ("Essays on Greek Literature," p. 39) thinks that "Hellas sprang from the blood of the Μαραθωνομάχαι." Grote says (Hist., vol. iii., p. 9) that the common action taken against Persia was "as near to a political union as Grecian temper would permit." Herodotus (vii. 148) speaks of οἱ συνωμόται Ἑλλήνων ἐπὶ τῷ Πέρσῃ. The Eginetans who gave earth and water to the emissary sent by Darius shortly before the Battle of Marathon were considered by both Athenians and Spartans to be "traitors to Greece" (προδόντες τὴν Ἑλλάδα) (Her., vi. 49). An account of the assembly—amounting almost to a Pan-Hellenic Congress—held under Athenian auspices in anticipation of the invasion of Xerxes, is given by Herodotus (vii. 145). An attempt made by Pericles, after the conclusion of the thirty-years' truce, to call a Pan-Hellenic Congress failed, owing, according to Plutarch ("Life of Pericles," Dryden's translation), to "the underhand crossing of the design" by the Lacedæmonians.

[2] Demosthenes says that when the Phocian War broke out the condition of the whole of Hellas was one of "strife

sitory and half-hearted alliances, intended to bind together by ropes of diplomatic sand the ephemeral interests of the various petty communities. The Greek nation had not yet been born. In spite of a common interest in Olympia, and in spite of the existence of the Amphictyonic Council, which, as Professor Freeman has pointed out,[1] was an Ecclesiastical Synod rather than a Federal Diet, the unit was still the πόλις.[2] "In respect to political sovereignty," Grote says,[3] "complete

and confusion." ἡ Πελοπόννησος ἅπασα διειστήκει, καὶ οὔθ' οἱ μισοῦντες Λακεδαιμονίους οὕτως ἴσχυον ὥστε ἀνελεῖν αὐτοὺς, οὔθ οἱ πρότερον δι' ἐκείνων ἄρχοντες κύριοι τῶν πόλεων ἦσαν, ἀλλά τις ἦν ἄκριτος καὶ παρὰ τούτοις καὶ παρὰ τοῖς ἄλλοις ἅπασιν ἔρις καὶ ταραχή (De Cor.).

[1] "History of Federal Government in Greece and Italy," p. 102.

[2] Curtius, however, dates the birth of the Greek nation from the creation of the Amphictyonic Council. "The most important result of all was that the members of the Amphictyony learnt to regard themselves as one united body against those standing outside it; out of a number of tribes arose a nation, which required a common name to distinguish it and its political and religious system from all other tribes" ("History of Greece," vol. i., p. 117). Grote's view (Hist., vol. ii., pp. 168-78, and vol. iii., p. 277) seems to be generally in harmony with that of Professor Freeman.

[3] Hist., vol. ii., p. 181.

disunion was amongst the most cherished principles" of the Greeks.

It is, however, unnecessary to labour this point. We must take the Athenian or Ionian, rather than the Dorian, as the typical Greek, and if we do so, it is almost a commonplace to state that the undisciplined and idealistic Greek, with his intense individuality, was far less suitable to carry an Imperial policy into execution than the austere and practical Roman, who not only made the law, but obeyed it, and who was surrounded from his cradle to his grave with associations calculated to foster Imperial tendencies. Virgil, who was an enthusiastic Imperialist, was probably a true representative of the Roman public opinion of his day. The very word παιδεύειν in Greek has a different signification to the Latin word *educare*.

Perforce, therefore, we turn to Rome, and here surely, if it be true that history is philosophy teaching by example, some useful lessons are to be learnt.[1]

[1] Beside the considerations to which allusion is made above, it is to be observed that it is almost impossible to establish any analogy between Athenian and Roman Imperialism. The object which each sought to attain, and

I wish to preface my remarks by saying that, in dealing with British Imperialism, I propose to leave the self-governing colonies alone. My reasons are threefold.

In the first place, I would point to the relative magnitude, as also to the difficulty, of the Imperial problem in the case of those possessions of the Crown in which the inhabitants are not bound to us by any racial or religious ties. Of the 410 million British subjects, constituting about one-fifth of the population of the globe, 44 millions reside in the United Kingdom. Of the remainder, only about 12½ millions at most are of European—and these by no means of exclusively British—stock, 305 millions are Asiatics, and 48 millions are Africans of various races. India alone may

---

still more the means adopted for attaining it, differed widely. The Athenians wished to establish independent or semi-independent communities in foreign countries. On the other hand, as Mr. Finlay remarks ("History of Greece," vol. i., pp. 88-89), "Roman civilization moved only in the train of the armies of Rome, and its progress was arrested when the career of conquest stopped. . . . Foreign colonization was adverse to all the prejudices of a Roman." British Imperialism has at different times been more or less based both on Athenian and on Roman principles.

be said to be about equal in area and population to the whole of Europe outside Russia.[1] It is, perhaps, not superfluous to draw attention to these stupendous figures. The importance of the conclusions to be deduced from them is, perhaps, occasionally somewhat overlooked.

In the second place, it may be said that, whilst the foundations on which the British Imperial policy of the future is to be based in Asia and in parts of Africa are still in process of being laid, those foundations already rest on a secure basis in so far as the self-governing colonies are concerned. It is true that some important issues still remain to be decided. The commercial relations between Great Britain and those colonies constitute one of the controversial questions of the day. Measures which by some are regarded as calculated to cement the union are regarded by others as likely to tend rather towards the disintegration of the Empire. Further, the question of Imperial defence, which Professor Beer, of Columbia University, thinks was " the rock on which the old Empire—that is to say,

[1] Seeley, "Expansion of England," p. 217.

the Empire which existed up to nearly the end of the eighteenth century—was shattered,"[1] is still not wholly decided. These exceptions do not, however, seriously invalidate the general statement that, in so far as the self-governing colonies are concerned, the Imperial problem has been solved. Lord Durham's epoch-making mission to Canada seventy years ago resulted in practical effect being given to the principle which had been rudely enforced by the revolt of the American colonies. From that time forth, the colonies have practically governed themselves.

In the third place, it is obvious that no very close or instructive analogy can be established between Rome in her relations with the provincials and Great Britain in its relations with the self-governing colonies. When the poet Claudian, in an oft-quoted passage,[2] said that Rome gave rights of citizenship to those whom she had conquered—*cives vocavit quos domuit*—he meant something very different to what we mean when we say that self-governing powers have been accorded to Canada, the Australian

[1] Beer, "British Colonial Policy, 1754-1765," p. 3.
[2] De Cons. Stil., iii. 152-53.

colonies, or South Africa. From a very early period of her history, Rome was frequently incorporating new bodies of citizens. At the commencement of the third century, Caracalla conferred the franchise on practically the whole Roman world. But this privilege, though valuable in some respects, did not carry with it any self-governing powers. It merely conferred on a very large number of provincials a personal right to vote in the Roman Assembly. The Roman system, in Professor Freeman's words, was "as if the Livery of London were invested with supreme power, every elector in the United Kingdom being at the same time invested with the freedom of the City."[1]

I turn, therefore, to a consideration of those British possessions on which self-governing powers, in the full sense of the term, have not been conferred. The great Imperial problem of the future is to what an extent some 350 millions of British subjects, who are aliens to us in race, religion, language, manners, and

[1] "History of Federal Government in Greece and Italy," p. 24. Augustus endeavoured to place Roman citizens resident in the Italian colonies on a footing of practical equality with those resident in Rome by enabling the former to transmit their votes in writing to Rome (Suet., Oct. c. 46).

customs, are to govern themselves, or are to be governed by us. Rome never had to face such an issue as this. Mr. Bryce estimates that the total population of the Roman Empire in the days of Trajan was at most 100 millions, spread over 2½ million square miles of country,[1] as compared to the 11½ million square miles over which the British flag flies.

The first points of analogy which must strike anyone who endeavours to institute a comparison between Roman and modern—notably British—Imperial policy are that in proceeding from conquest to conquest each step in advance was in ancient, as it has been in modern, times accompanied by misgivings, and was often taken with a reluctance which was by no means feigned; that Rome, equally with the modern expansive Powers, more especially Great Britain and Russia, was impelled onwards by the imperious and

[1] "Studies in History and Jurisprudence," vol. i., p. 17. Mr. Fynes Clinton ("Fasti Hellenici," vol. i., p. 603) gives the total extent of the Roman Empire, exclusive of the Tauric Chersonese and the northern shore of the Euxine, as 1,636,398 square miles

irresistible necessity of acquiring defensible frontiers; that the public opinion of the world scoffed 2,000 years ago, as it does now, at the alleged necessity; and that each onward move was attributed to an insatiable lust for an extended dominion.[1]

The Roman policy of world-conquest may be said to have been inaugurated by the First Punic War, in B.C. 264-241.[2] It received a great stimulus from the campaigns of Lucullus (B.C. 73), who, Mr. Ferrero says,[3] " introduced a new conception into Roman policy—the

[1] It is estimated that during the ten years from 1879 to 1889 there was an increase of British territory throughout the world of some 1,250,000 square miles, or about one-third of the area of Europe. On this, Sir Charles Lucas (Preface to Lewis's "Government of Dependencies," p. xix) remarks: "A policy of annexation has been forced upon Great Britain during the last half-century, and has certainly not been lightly entered into by her Government or her people; but the result has been the same as if she had been simply bent upon wholesale aggrandizement."

[2] τῷ γὰρ πολέμῳ κρατήσαντες Ῥωμαῖοι Καρχηδονίων, καὶ νομίσαντες τὸ κυριώτατον καὶ μέγιστον μέρος αὑτοῖς ἠνύσθαι πρὸς τὴν τῶν ὅλων ἐπιβολήν, οὕτω καὶ τότε πρῶτον ἐθάρσησαν ἐπὶ τὰ λοιπὰ τὰς χεῖρας ἐκτείνειν, καὶ περαιοῦσθαι μετὰ δυνάμεων εἴς τε τὴν Ἑλλάδα καὶ τοὺς κατὰ τὴν Ἀσίαν τόπους (Polyb., i. 3).

[3] Ferrero, "The Greatness and Decline of Rome," vol. i., p. 151.

idea of aggressive Imperialism." It paused, though it did not terminate, with the battle of Actium (B.C. 31) and the capture of Egypt. During this long period, constant but ineffectual efforts were made, either by corporate bodies or individuals, to stem the ever-advancing tide of conquest. Scipio and the Roman aristocracy were persistently averse to an extension of empire. This view was shared by the Senate—at all events, up to the time of the Macedonian defeat at Pydna (B.C. 168). Cato, to use a term which is now at times woefully misapplied, was a "little Roman," though his views may have been dictated by a fear lest extension should bring in its train an accession of that demoralizing Greek influence which was so repugnant to his sturdy conservatism, rather than by any doubts as to the wisdom of the policy on other grounds. In B.C. 27 Augustus, who was aware that the power of Rome was limited as compared to its prestige, endeavoured to evade the popular cry in favour of a Parthian war. Even so late as the days of Trajan and Adrian, the historian Florus expressed grave doubts as to whether it would not have been better to be content with Sicily and Africa, "or even to have been without them," rather than that Rome should grow to such greatness as to be ruined by her own strength.[1]

The Romans, therefore—or, at all events, some of the wisest amongst them—struggled as honestly and manfully to check the appetite for self-aggrandizement as ever Mr. Gladstone and Lord Granville strove to shake off the Egyptian burthen in 1882. Rather than attempt to rule direct, they resorted, as in the case of the Numidian Masinissa, to the policy of buffer states, with the result, in this particular instance, that before long they had to wage a serious war against Jugurtha, the

[1] "Ac nescio an satius fuerit populo Romano Sicilia et Africa contento fuisse, aut his etiam ipsis parcere dominanti in Italia sua, quam eo magnitudinis crescere ut uiribus suis conficeretur" (Florus, Epit., I. xlvi.).

Lucan, speaking of the extent of the Roman Empire, says:

"Quo latius orbem
Possedit citius per prospera fata cucurrit.
Omne tibi bellum gentes dedit omnibus annis:
Te geminum Titan procedere vidit in axem;
Haud multum terræ spatium restabat Eoæ,
Ut tibi nox tibi tota dies tibi curreret æther,
Omniaque errantes stellæ Romana viderent."
(Phars., vii. 419.)

ANCIENT AND MODERN IMPERIALISM 23

grandson of the vassal whom they had set up. They adopted, in the first instance, a similar policy in Asia Minor. Though reluctantly forced into war by Antiochus the Great, they took nothing for themselves at the conclusion of the peace which followed upon the crushing defeat inflicted on that ambitious monarch at Magnesia (B.C. 188). They merely substituted the authority of the Pergamene for that of the Seleucid dynasty. Augustus, although in attempting to conquer Germany he undertook a policy of expansion and direct government of a limited character, fell back in Asia Minor on the creation of buffer states, which, in spite of the death-blow given by Pompey to the system of protectorates after the Mithridatic Wars (B.C. 65-63), lasted till the time of Vespasian. He refused to annex Armenia on the murder of its King, Artaxes,[1] whom Tiberius had been sent to depose, although, according to his own statement, he could have done so.[2]

[1] ". . . Claudi virtute Neronis Armenius cecidit" (Hor., Ep. I., xii. 26).

[2] Arnold, "Studies of Roman Imperialism," p. 213. Mr. Arnold bases his statement on a quotation from the Monumentum Ancyranum. Similarly, in 1765, Clive

All these efforts to check the rising tide of Imperialism were in vain. Perhaps they were not always very whole-hearted. Reluctance to assume further responsibilities was constantly struggling both with national pride, which urged that those responsibilities should be assumed, and with fear of the consequences if some really efficient ruler were allowed to take in hand the task which Rome had declined.

At the death of Antiochus IV. (Epiphanes) in B.C. 164, his nephew, Demetrius the Saviour, was residing at Rome, whither he had been brought as a hostage some years previously. Though his character subsequently degenerated, he was at that time a youth who gave remarkably good promise for the future. He had from his childhood been surrounded by Roman associations. He was known to be popular in Syria. Here, therefore, was a good opportunity for the Roman Government, had it wished to do so, to take a really effective step in the direction of shaking off Imperial burdens, and placing them on the shoulders of one who, though not a Roman, was believed

---

refused to annex Oudh at the conclusion of a successful campaign.

to be a sympathizer with Rome. But the Senate evidently preferred that their vassals should be nonentities rather than effective rulers. They refused the appeal made by Demetrius that he should be allowed to return to his native country. With the connivance of his compatriot Polybius, he escaped,[1] and it was only by the bestowal of very liberal presents that he eventually obtained from the Romans his recognition as King.

Many potent and often uncontrollable forces were, in fact, persistently acting in the direction of expansion. Ambitious proconsuls and commanders—the prototypes of the British Warren Hastings and the Russian Skobeleff—who were animated either by personal motives or by a strong conviction of the necessity of action in Roman interests, were constantly forcing the hands of the central Government. Such, amongst numerous examples which might be cited, were Lucullus (B.C. 72)[2]

[1] Polybius, xxxi. 20-23. A graphic account of this episode is given in Bevan's " House of Seleucus " (vol. ii., c. xxvii.).

[2] " If the favourable opportunity was to be employed, and Armenia was to be dealt with in earnest, Lucullus had to begin the war, without any proper orders from the

and Aquilius (B.C. 89)[1] in Asia Minor, and Gallus (B.C. 27)[2] in Egypt. Moreover, not only was it a "supreme principle of the Roman Government to acknowledge no frontier Power with equal rights"[3]—a principle the execution of which manifestly tended to an extension of territory until the sea-coast or some other natural boundary was reached; not only were the Romans at times compelled to

---

Senate, at his own hand and his own risk. He found himself, just like Sulla, placed under the necessity of executing what he did in the most manifest interest of the existing Government, not with its sanction, but in spite of it" (Mommsen, "History of Rome," vol. iv., p. 335). Mr. Ferrero ("Characters and Events of Roman History," p. 18) calls Lucullus "the strongest man in the history of Rome."

[1] "Although neither the Roman Senate nor King Mithridates had desired the rupture, Aquilius desired it, and war ensued" (Mommsen, "History of Rome," vol. iv., p. 29).

[2] "While Gallus was undoubtedly anxious to satisfy his own wish for glory and plunder, he was no doubt equally anxious to impress the Egyptians with the new government, and to convince them of its greater severity and vigour compared with the rule of the Ptolemies. . . . Thus Gallus, undisturbed by the authority of the Senate or of Augustus, acted in Egypt precisely as he pleased" (Ferrero, "The Greatness and Decline of Rome," vol. iv., p. 170).

[3] Mommsen, "The Provinces of the Roman Empire," vol. ii., p. 51.

occupy a country in order to prevent others from occupying it, as has repeatedly occurred in the history of British Imperialism;[1] but one at least of their greatest statesmen and administrators advocated a forward policy on the ground that it would be impolitic to allow the subjects of Rome to run the risk of contamination by close contact with a free people. Agricola urged the necessity of occupying Ireland in order to overawe the Britons by surrounding them with Roman arms, and thus, as it were, " banish liberty from their sight."[2]

[1] " We may find a not too fanciful analogy to the policy of the English in the days of Clive, when they were drawn farther and farther into Indian conflicts by their efforts to check the enterprises of Dupleix and Lally, in the policy of the Romans when they entered Sicily to prevent Carthage from establishing her control over it " (Bryce, " Studies, etc.," vol. i., p. 9).

" The new British annexations in Africa have been made, not so much because there was a strong desire in England to take more of Africa, as because, if it had not been taken by the English, it might or would have been by the Germans " (Lucas's Preface to Lewis's " Government of Dependencies," p. xxi).

[2] " Sæpe ex eo audivi legione una et modicis auxiliis debellari obtinerique Hiberniam posse ; idque etiam adversus Britanniam profuturum, si Romana ubique arma et velut e conspectu libertas tolleretur " (Tacitus, Agric., c. 24).

Again, the acute dissensions amongst the neighbouring tribes materially contributed in the case of Rome, as it did in the case of the British in India, and of the Russians in Central Asia and the Caucasus,[1] towards the execution of an Imperial policy. Instances abound. One Gallic tribe constantly asked for Roman assistance to crush another. Adherbal made an

[1] Mr. Baddeley ("The Russian Conquest of the Caucasus," p. 295) gives a striking instance which occurred in 1837. The chief of one of the tribes in the Caucasus addressed his followers in the following terms: "Avars! Rather than that these dogs of Murids should rob and ruin us, will it not be better to call in the Russians? They will not occupy our houses nor take away our last crust of bread. They are brave and generous, and so far have never been ashamed to have to do with poor, simple folk like us. Why should we avoid them? For whose sake? Will it not be better to dwell in the closest alliance with them? We shall be rich, peaceful, and then let us see who will dare to insult us!"

In India the idea of utilizing internal dissensions in order to assert European supremacy was first originated by Dupleix.

The danger of calling in a powerful and ambitious neighbour to help in the suppression of internal discord was fully realized by some, at all events, of the Greek states. The address which Hermocrates delivered to the Sicilians (Thuc., iv. 59-64) dwells strongly on the danger to all Sicily which would be involved in invoking aid from Athens.

eloquent appeal to the Roman Senate for help against Jugurtha.[1] Rome was invited to become the champion of Hellenic freedom in Asia Minor, and when the invitation had been accepted, and help effectively given, it was soon found, in the words of Mommsen, that "the most detestable form of Macedonian rule was less fraught with evil for Greece than a free constitution springing from the noblest intentions of honourable foreigners."[2] It is, indeed, one of the inevitable incidents of the execution of an Imperial policy that, as a political force, the gratitude shown to the foreigner who relieves oppression is of a very ephemeral character. We have learnt this lesson both in India and in Egypt. The French also have learnt it in Algiers and Cochin China, the Russians in Central Asia.[3]

[1] "Patres conscripti, per vos per liberos atque parentes, per majestatem populi Romani, subvenite misero mihi; ite obviam injuriæ; nolite pati regnum Numidiæ, quod vestrum est, per scelus et sanguinem familiæ nostræ tabescere (Sallust, Jugurtha, xiv.).

[2] Mommsen, "History of Rome," vol. ii., p. 494.

[3] Mr. Rice Holmes ("History of the Indian Mutiny," p. 557) quotes from Sir George Campbell's Memoirs a passage from a letter written by a Sepoy officer, and discovered in the palace of Delhi, in which it is stated that,

## 30  ANCIENT AND MODERN IMPERIALISM

The Roman Imperialists were not slow to take advantage of the opportunities thus afforded to them. No scruples of conscience deterred them from applying to its fullest extent the celebrated, albeit cynical, maxim of Machiavelli. They endeavoured to divide and govern. The most illustrious of their historians did not hesitate to record a pious hope that the nations of the world would retain and perpetuate, if not an affection for Rome, at least an animosity against each other;[1] and Tiberius pointed out to Ger-

---

"with all the faults of the English, their government was the best Hindostan has ever seen." But he also quotes a statement made by Lord Lawrence to the effect that "the people of India can never forget that we are an alien race in respect of colour, religion, habits, and sympathies." This really sums up all there is to be said on the subject. *Mutatis mutandis*, Lord Lawrence's dictum may be applied to Egypt, Algeria, Tunis, Annam, the Asiatic provinces of Russia, and, in fact, to every country where the Western governs the Eastern. History in this matter repeats itself. Gregorovius ("Rome in the Middle Ages," vol. i., p. 327), speaking of the rule of Theodosius in Italy, says: "The unhappy King now learnt by experience that not even the wisest or most humane of Princes, if he be an alien in race, in customs, and religion, can ever win the hearts of the people."

[1] " Maneat, quæso, duretque gentibus, si non amor nostri, at certe odium sui, quando urguentibus imperii fatis nihil

manicus, as an inducement for him to return to Italy, that the most politic method of treating the German tribes was to leave them to cut each other's throats.[1]

All these were, however, but contributory causes. It cannot be doubted that it was the desire to obtain natural and defensible frontiers in all directions which gave the main stimulus to Roman expansion. In Gaul, Spain, and Numidia such a frontier was provided by either the ocean or the desert; but it was wanting elsewhere. "The North and the East," Mr. Bryce very truly says, "ultimately destroyed Rome."[2] It was from these quarters that the Teuton and the Slav poured in, and marched to what was pathetically, but very erroneously, thought by a fifth-century Roman[3] to be "the funeral of the world."

---

iam præstare fortuna maius potest quam hostium discordiam" (Tacitus, De Ger., 33).

[1] "Posse et Cheruscos ceterasque rebellium gentes, quoniam Romanæ ultioni consultum esset, internis discordiis relinqui" (Tacitus, Ann., ii. 26).

[2] "Studies, etc.," p. 15.

[3] Sidonius Apollinaris. Besides the Teuton and the Slav, the Persians contributed to the work of destruction. The crushing defeat inflicted by the Persians on the Emperor Valerian (A.D. 259 or 260) gave a death-blow to Roman domination in the East.

The same motive impelled the British trading company, which had been empowered in 1686 to "make peace and war with the heathen nations"[1] of India, to move onwards until they or the British Government, which eventually took over their governing powers, reached the barrier of the Himalayas, and, when these had been reached, to ask themselves wistfully whether even that frontier was sufficiently secure. Similarly, the Russians were driven across the steppes of Central Asia, and the French in Algeria from the sea-coast to the confines of the Great Sahara.

It can be no matter for surprise that both the ancient and the modern world, prompted in the case of the victims by actual loss of wealth and position, and in the case of others by fear mingled with jealousy, should have condemned the policy of expansion, and should have refused to take seriously the excuse proffered for its adoption. Mithridates inveighed against "the insatiable desire for empire and wealth" displayed by the Romans,[2]

[1] Ilbert, "The Government of India," p. 31. The first charter was granted in 1600.
[2] Letter to King Arsaces, Sallust.

and many years later the British chief Calgacus uttered a similar protest in a speech in which he is alleged to have made use of the world-famous phrase, *Ubi solitudinem faciunt, pacem appellant.*[1] British Imperial policy has in modern times been assailed with criticism which, if not similar in detail, has been no less vehement, whilst we ourselves have at times, with some inconsistency, attributed Russian advance in Central Asia solely to ambition, and have waived aside all explanations based on the necessities of the situation.[2]

A somewhat close analogy may, therefore, be established between the motive power which impelled both ancient and modern Imperialists onwards.

[1] Tacitus, Agric., 30.
[2] Terentyeff ("Russia and England in Central Asia," vol. ii., p. 153) says: "Our movements in the East are not the result of any premeditated plan, but have been the immediate consequence of the necessities of the moment." Raids, encouraged by the activity of some bold frontier chieftain, have largely contributed to stimulate an aggressive policy, both in ancient and in modern times. Tacfarinas in Numidia was the political precursor of Abd-el-Kader in Algeria, and of many who have opposed the advance of Russia in Asia—*e.g.*, Schamyl in the Caucasus.

Their methods were also very similar. In both cases undaunted audacity characterized their proceedings. Sulla (B.C. 86) did not hesitate to give battle at Chæronea to an army three times as numerous as his own, sent against him by Mithridates, with the result that he gained a complete victory. A Roman Centurion of the Tenth Legion, when taken prisoner, boldly stated that with ten of his men he would beat 500 of the enemy.[1] With a mere handful of troops, Clive won the Battle of Plassy and founded the Indian Empire.[2] There is, in fact, a good deal of similarity between the Roman and British character. Both nations appear to the best advantage in critical times. Polybius said

[1] Mommsen, "History of Rome," vol. v., p. 198.

[2] Similar instances might be quoted in connection with the Russian conquest of Central Asia. "At the capture of Tashkend, under Chernajeff, 1,500 Russians opposed 15,000 Khokandian troops and 90,000 hostile natives" (Vambéry, "Western Culture in Eastern Lands," p. 152). Perhaps the most striking instances of audacity in the execution of an Imperial policy are to be found in the history of the foundation of the Spanish South American Empire (see, *inter alia*, Prescott's "Conquest of Peru," vol. i., pp. 327, 340, 360, and "Conquest of Mexico," vol. i., pp. 216, 321).

that the Romans were most to be feared when their danger was greatest.[1] I well remember being struck by the slight effect produced in Egypt by our early reverses during the recent South African War. All were convinced that we were the inheritors of that proud motto which laid down as a principle of policy that Rome should never make peace save as a victor. Even amongst hostile critics, warm admiration was excited by the steadfastness shown by the nation under trial —an admiration, I should add, which was somewhat qualified by the delirious and undignified rejoicings which took place when the main danger was past.

In respect to another point, the methods employed by the British, both in India and in Egypt, bear a striking similarity to that adopted by the Romans. Both nations have been largely aided by auxiliaries drawn from the countries which they conquered. The Romans were driven to resort to this expedient owing to the paucity of their own numbers compared to the extent of their

[1] Polybius, i. 20, 59.

dominions, and to the unpopularity of foreign service amongst their own troops.[1] Economy and convenience led the British, alone amongst modern expanding Powers, to follow their example on a large scale.[2] Sir John Seeley says: "The nations of India have been conquered by an army of which, on the average, about a fifth were English."[3]

The employment of auxiliaries on a large

[1] "The Roman burgesses began to perceive that dominion over a foreign people is an annoyance not only to the slave, but to the master, and murmured loudly regarding the odious war-service of Spain. While the new Generals, with good reason, refused to allow the relief of the existing corps as a whole, the men mutinied and threatened that, if they were not allowed their discharge, they would take it of their own accord" (Mommsen, "History of Rome," vol. ii., p. 389).

[2] The system was not initiated by the British. We copied it from the French. Colonel Chesney ("Indian Polity") says: "The first establishment of the Company's Indian Army may be considered to date from the year 1748, when a small body of Sepoys was raised at Madras, after the example set by the French for the defence of that settlement."

The French still employ auxiliary troops in Algeria, but on a far smaller scale than ourselves. With the exception of a few Turcoman irregular horse, the whole of the so-called "Asiatic Army" of Russia is composed of Russians.

[3] "Expansion of England," p. 233.

scale is a bold and somewhat hazardous experiment. It would appear, of necessity, to lead to one of two consequences: either the conquered race is ultimately placed on an equal—or even, possibly, on a superior—footing to its conquerors, or else the subject race acquiesces in its subjection, and loyally co-operates with its alien rulers. The first of these two consequences ensued to Rome. To give only a few illustrations which occurred at various periods before Rome was finally overwhelmed by the northern flood: Trajan, Marcus Aurelius, and Seneca were Spaniards. Septimius Severus belonged to a Gallic family, and was born in Africa. Neither was the equality, which eventually drifted into superiority, confined to the world of politics. The poet Martial, at a time when Roman Imperialism was mainly represented by those who were not merely in name, but in fact, Romans, boasted of his Spanish birth.[1] The rhetorician, Quintilian, who preceded Martial by a few years, was possibly a Spaniard, and

---

[1] "Ex Hiberis
Et Celtis genitus Tagique civis" (x. 65).

was certainly born in Spain. Terence was a Carthaginian slave.

No such consequences, or anything at all like them, have ensued in the case of Great Britain. With the exception of a passing, and not very important, political episode towards the close of the eighteenth century, when India added its drop to the existing ocean of Parliamentary corruption, it may be said that the Indian connection, although it has widely influenced British policy, has not in any degree influenced the composition of the legislative and executive machine through whose agency that policy has been directed.

Can it be said with truth that the alternative consequence has ensued—that the subject races have acquiesced in their subjection, and that the auxiliary troops recruited from amongst those races have loyally co-operated with their alien rulers? The great Mutiny which occurred in India some fifty years ago would, at first sight, appear to supply a negative answer to this question; yet the answer would be by no means conclusive, for the conclusion must obviously depend upon the reasons which led up to the events of 1857.

Political causes, without doubt, contributed to produce the result.[1] Yet, in spite of the opposite opinion expressed by one of the historians of the Sepoy war,[2] I believe that

[1] It can, I think, scarcely be doubted that the adoption of the policy of "annexations by lapse" was the most important of these political causes. This matter is fully discussed in Sir William Lee-Warner's "Life of the Marquis of Dalhousie" (vol. ii., chap. v.). Although Lord Dalhousie was an active agent in the execution of the policy of annexation by lapse, he did not, as is often supposed, initiate it. So early as 1834, the Court of Directors wrote to the Governor-General: "Wherever it is optional with you to give or withhold your consent to adoption, the indulgence should be the exception and not the rule, and should never be granted but as a special mark of approbation." Sir Charles Wood (afterwards Lord Halifax), when President of the Board of Control, seems to have doubted the wisdom of the policy. In April, 1854, he wrote to Lord Dalhousie: "I am by no means impatient to absorb all these States, though I suppose it will come to this in the end."

[2] Malleson, "The Indian Mutiny," vol. iii., p. 470, *et seq.* The causes which led up to the Mutiny are very fully stated by Mr. Rice Holmes in his "History of the Indian Mutiny." A summary is given on pp. 556-60. The main point to bear in mind is that the British Government, in 1857, had, broadly speaking, to deal, not with a general rising of the population, but with a mutiny. "The disturbances," Mr. Rice Holmes says (p. 558), "except in one or two isolated regions, and on the part of a few embittered or fanatical

Lord Lawrence was right in regarding the whole of this episode mainly as a military mutiny rather than a political movement. Nor should it ever be forgotten that, even during that time of stress and convulsion, no inconsiderable body of the auxiliary troops remained loyal. Throughout the length and breadth of the British Empire there exists no monument of greater political significance than that erected by Lord Northbrook at Lucknow in honour of the heroism of those Sepoys who, in the face of temptations which would have rendered defection, to say the least, excusable, adhered to the British cause.

If we leave aside the episode of the Mutiny, the answer to the question I have propounded cannot be doubtful. On many a well-fought field, not only the bravery, but also the loyalty, of the auxiliary troops of Great Britain have been conspicuous.

Will the past be repeated in the future? Will the steadfast loyalty, to which both the rulers and the ruled may look with equal pride

---

groups, never amounted to a rebellion." I think that this verdict will be endorsed by most of those who know India, and who have studied this particular question.

and satisfaction, resist those disintegrating forces now being stimulated into action, both in India and England, with a recklessness which at times seems to take but little heed of that wise old saw, *Respice finem?* That is one of the crucial Imperial questions of the future. I will not hazard a prophecy about it.

An Imperial Power naturally expects to derive some benefits for itself from its Imperialism. There can be no doubt as to the quarter to which the Romans looked for their profit. They exacted heavy tributes from their dependencies.[1] They regarded the pro-

[1] The Athenians adopted a similar system. At the height of their empire there were, according to Aristophanes (Vesp., 696), one thousand cities tributary to Athens. These are believed to have paid collectively an annual tribute of 600 talents (about £150,000). The tribute was subsequently commuted, or perhaps it would be more correct to say increased (Thuc., vii. 28), to a 5 per cent. *ad valorem* duty on all imports and exports. Little seems to be known as to the incidence of the tribute on each city (see Grote's "Hist.," vol. iv., p. 492), but there can be no doubt that the tribute constituted the main source of Athenian revenue. Boeckh ("Public Economy of Athens," Lewis's translation, p. 396) says: "By far the most productive source of revenue belonging to the Athenian State was the tributes (φόροι) of the allies."

vinces solely from the point of view of the revenue which could be obtained from them.[1] The onerous nature of the tribute may best be realized by giving the facts relating to Egypt. Under Ptolemy Philadelphus, 6¾ million modii of corn were annually collected in Egypt. Under Augustus, the quantity sent to Rome was no less than 20 millions of modii. In other words, instead of a tax amounting to £180,000, all of which was spent in the country, no less than £531,000 was levied and

---

Pericles (Thuc., ii. 13) advised his countrymen to keep a tight hand over the allies (τά τε τῶν ξυμμάχων διὰ χειρὸς ἔχειν), because their main strength was derived from the tribute. The *quid pro quo* which the tributaries received to compensate them for the onerous burdens which they had to bear was that the Ægean was cleared of Persian ships.

[1] "Les provinces sont des *prædia* du peuple romain, et leur importance au point de vue de l'État réside uniquement dans les revenus qu'elles lui fournissent" (Marquardt, "Organisation de l'Empire Romain," vol. ii., p. 558). "Le peuple dominateur vécut du revenu des provinces comme un propriétaire du produit de ses immeubles" (Marquardt, "L'Organisation Financière chez les Romains," p. 189). One of the principal functions of the procurators in the imperial, and the quæstors in the senatorial, provinces was to exact the full and punctual payment of the tribute.

sent to Rome, exclusive of what was exacted for internal requirements.[1]

Although the methods adopted by the British in India differed widely from those of the Romans, the principle which they sought, in the first instance, to enforce was much the same. For all practical purposes it may be said that for some years India paid a tribute to Great Britain. The trade of the East India Company was at first enormously lucrative. In 1622, goods bought in India for £356,000 sold for £1,915,000 in England.[2] The result was that the Company, besides making at times large loans to the British Government, were able to pay an annual tribute of £400,000 to the Treasury. The main reason which, in 1763, decided the contest between France and England for the possession of India in favour of the latter Power was unquestionably its predominance as a maritime Power. But a subsidiary cause, which contributed in no small

[1] Wilcken, "Griechische Ostraka," vol. i., p. 421, and Marquardt's "Organisation Financière," p. 294. I have, on the authority of Marquardt, taken the price of a modius (about two English gallons) at 3 sesterces: 1,000 sesterces were equivalent to £8 17s. 1d.

[2] Lyall, "British Dominion in India," p. 20.

degree to the final result, was that, whereas in England the traders were able to pay the Government, in France the Government was called upon to pay large subsidies to the traders.[1] Hopes began to be entertained that some portion of the burthen of British taxation would be shifted to Indian shoulders.[2] Fortunately, these hopes were not realized. The system was abandoned in 1773, not, apparently, from any doubt as to its soundness, but by reason of the financial embarrassments of the Company, due to the great Bengal famine of 1770 and other causes, which rendered the continuance of the heavy pay-

[1] " Quant aux ressources de finance, il est notoire que l'imposition que l'on lève dans nos Colonies ne suffit pas à beaucoup près aux dépenses de sûreté et d'administration qu'elles entrainent" ("Œuvres de Turgot," viii. 459, cited by Lewis, "Government of Dependencies," p. 207). The French over-sea possessions still constitute a drain on the French Treasury. According to "The Statesman's Year-Book for 1909" (p. 790), the total expenditure in Algeria, including military and extraordinary disbursements, is about £3,000,000 in excess of the revenue.

[2] "Alderman Beckford expressed in the House of Commons his hope that the rich acquisitions of the Company in the East would be made a means of relieving the people of England from some of their burdens" (Lyall, "British Dominion, etc.," p. 172).

ments of former years impossible. Whatever may have been the causes, the change was eminently beneficial, for the system, though not so faulty as that formerly adopted by the Spaniards towards their American colonies,[1] was, both politically and economically, thoroughly unsound. From 1773 onwards, England has regarded trade with India, and not tribute from India, as the financial asset which counterbalances the burthen of governing the country.

In judging of the methods employed by ancient and modern Imperialists to effect the objects which they respectively had in view, it is not easy to avoid doing some injustice to the former. Christianity has intervened between the two periods, and has established a moral code on principles almost wholly unknown to the ancient world, although to the Stoics may be awarded the merit of having paved the way for the humanitarianism of the

[1] The Spanish colonies were obliged to export the precious metals, but were forbidden to receive commodities in exchange from the mother-country. Thus the whole of the colonial trade fell into the hands of other nations.

Christian.[1] Professor Bury, if I understand rightly, thinks that the public morality of the Romans was superior to that of the Greeks;[2] and there can, I venture to think, be little doubt that this view is correct. The speeches which Thucydides put into the mouths of his orators, if those speeches can

[1] "It was the Stoics in the earlier Imperial times who first rose to the conception of humanity and of human, as distinct from local and national, rights. . . . The Stoic and the Christian were the first humanitarians" (Laurie, "Historical Survey of Pre-Christian Education," p. 8. See also on this subject Dill's "Roman Society from Nero to Marcus Aurelius," p. 307 et seq., and Glover's "Conflict of Religions in the Early Roman Empire," chap. ii.). Professor Sonnenschein, in an article published in the *National Review* of June, 1906, gives strong reasons for holding that Shakespeare drew from Seneca (De Clem.) the essential ideas of the celebrated speech on mercy in "The Merchant of Venice." According to a high authority, the Stoics were also to some extent the fathers of modern economic science. Professor Marshall ("Principles of Economics," vol. i., p. 733) says: "To Roman, and especially Stoic, influence we may trace indirectly much of the good and evil of our present economic system; on the one hand, much of the untrammelled vigour of the individual in managing his own affairs, and, on the other, not a little harsh wrong done under the cover of rights established by a system of law which has held its ground because its main principles are wise and just."

[2] Bury, "The Ancient Greek Historians," p. 143.

be taken as true indications of contemporary opinion, abound in statements indicative of the " false moral arithmetic "—to use a phrase which, I think, is Bentham's—current at his time; as, for instance, when an Athenian envoy, speaking to the Lacedæmonians, urged that " Men who indulge the rational ambition of empire deserve credit if they are in any degree more careful of justice than they need be."[1]

On the other hand, Tacitus, like Sallust, "would not acknowledge that the standard applied in private conduct may be inapplicable to public transactions "[2]—a high ideal, to which

[1] Thuc., i. 76.
[2] Bury, "The Ancient Greek Historians," p. 271. Mr. Butcher has drawn my attention to the fact that a similar code of high morality was inculcated by Demosthenes. In Olynth. ii., 10, he said: " It is not possible, Athenians, it is not possible to found a solid power upon oppression, perjury, and falsehood. Such an empire may endure for the moment or for the hour; nay, it may, perhaps, blossom with the rich promise of hope, but time finds it out, and it drops away of itself. As in a house, a vessel, or any similar structure, the foundations should above all be strong, so should the principles and groundwork of conduct rest upon truth and justice." And in his speech against Leptines, § 136, Demosthenes expressed himself in the following terms: " Beware not to exhibit as a nation conduct which you would shrink from as individuals."

even the Christian world, in spite of the efforts of statesmen such as Burke and Bright, has not yet attained.[1] But although a few eminent men, who were greatly in advance of their day, may have cherished lofty ideals of this description, I conceive that they did not in any way correctly represent the public opinion of the mass of their contemporaries. It would, indeed, be unjust to judge of the general tenor of that opinion by a few isolated episodes. If, for instance, it be urged that the bleeding head of the vanquished general Crassus was used as a stage accessory in the performance of the Bacchæ "to the infinite delight of an audience of half-Hellenized barbarians,"[2] it may be replied that posterity will greatly err if it judges of the civilization of the eighteenth century by the conduct of Le Bon, Carrier, and other monsters of the

[1] "Nothing is more calamitous than the divorce of politics from morals, but in practical politics public and private morals will never absolutely correspond" (Lecky, "Map of Life," p. 181). Lord Acton ("Historical Essays," p. 506), with his usual felicity of statement, puts the case thus: "The principles of public morality are as definite as those of the morality of private life, but they are not identical."

[2] Mommsen, "History, etc.," vol. v., p. 162.

## ANCIENT AND MODERN IMPERIALISM    49

French Revolution. Traces of the existence of a humanitarian policy are, indeed, to be found in the records of Roman Imperialism. The cruelties of Druidical worship, which were left untouched by Julius Cæsar, were suppressed by Claudius,[1] although in this instance the humanitarian action was possibly dictated by the political consideration that nationalism drew its main element of strength from religion.[2] The policy of Augustus in the East was "mild, just, and conciliatory."[3] So also was that of Agricola in Britain,[4] and that of the Antonines at a later period throughout the empire.[5]

[1] Suet., Vita Claud., c. 15. Alexander, when in Bactria, suppressed some very inhuman local practices connected with Zoroastrianism (Bevan, "The House of Seleucus," i. 290).

[2] Mommsen ("Provinces of the Roman Empire," vol. i., p. 105) says: "That direct opposition to the foreign rule prevailed in the Druidism of this period cannot be proved." But he appears to think that its existence was highly probable.

[3] Ferrero, "Greatness and Decline, etc.," iv. 241.

[4] Tacitus, Agric., c. 27.

[5] "Procuratores suos modeste suscipere tributa jussit: excedentes modum, rationem factorum suorum reddere præcepit: nec unquam lætatus est lucro quo provincialis oppressus est. Contra procuratores suos conquerentes libenter audivit" (Julius Capitolinus, Antonini Pii Vita, c. vi.).

Moreover, contact with the cultured mind of Greece must have exercised, and certainly did exercise, some humanizing influence on Roman thought.[1] In spite, however, of these palliating circumstances, it may be said that Roman Imperial policy, even after the reforms introduced during the early years of the empire, if judged by such modern standards as we are wont to apply, stands condemned. This is, I think, now very generally recognized, and by no one more so than by the most recent historian of Rome. "We must," Mr. Ferrero says, "abandon one of the most general and most widespread misconceptions,[2] which teaches

---

[1] Greece was the last of the Roman provinces into which gladiatorial games were introduced, and their introduction was effected under protest from some who fitly represented the true Greek spirit of culture and humanity. "One of the best (amongst the Athenians) asked his countrymen whether they might not first set up an altar to the God of compassion, and several of the noblest turned indignantly away from the city of their fathers that so dishonoured itself" ("Provinces of the Roman Empire," i. 172). Seneca, as is well known, protested against the gladiatorial shows, but it was not till paganism had succumbed to Christianity that they were finally abolished (A.D. 325).

[2] The opposite view to that entertained by Mr. Ferrero is thus expressed by Professor Gwatkin ("Early Church

that Rome administered her provinces in a broad-minded spirit, consulting the general interest, and adopting wide and beneficent principles of government for the good of the subjects."[1] Very great improvements were, indeed, made by Augustus. Like all who have had to encounter the practical difficulties of administrative work, he found that the first and most essential step towards the creation of a sound administration was to establish an efficient Department of Accounts,[2]

---

History to A.D. 313," p. 52): "She [Rome] was the first of the Great Empires, and almost the only one to our own time, which turned subjects into citizens, and ruled them for their own good, and not for selfish gain."

[1] "Greatness and Decline, etc.," vol. v., p. 3. The rule of the Carthaginians over their dependencies was even more oppressive than that of the Romans. Polybius (i. 72) says that the Carthaginian Governors, who were considered the most efficient, were those who, like Hanno, levied the largest tribute, and employed the harshest measures for levying it, and not those who dealt mildly and humanely with the people. The discontent caused by these measures led the dependencies to take part against the Carthaginians in the First Punic War.

[2] It would be difficult to exaggerate the importance of this point. The establishment of a proper system of accounts must necessarily precede the inception and execution of any sound financial policy; and the inaugura-

and accordingly he introduced a system, which was subsequently improved by Hadrian and Vespasian, and which, according to a highly qualified modern authority,[1] formed the original basis of all subsequent systems. He discovered

---

tion of a sound financial policy is the necessary and indispensable precursor of all moral and material progress in backward Oriental states. It is to be hoped that this commonplace truth will be fully realized by the reformers at Constantinople, whose proceedings are now being watched with so much sympathetic interest in this country. I have dwelt on this subject, in so far as Egypt is concerned, in " Modern Egypt," vol. i., pp. 26-28.

It is certain that one, and perhaps not the least formidable, of the difficulties which had to be encountered by the statesmen who, in the early days of Louis XVI., endeavoured ineffectually to stem the tide of the Revolution was that the French accounts were at that time in such confusion that it was almost impossible to ascertain the true facts with which the Minister of Finance had to deal. This is strongly brought out in the " Requête au Roi," addressed by M. de Calonne to the King in 1787. Chérest ("La Chute de l'Ancien Régime," vol. i., p. 83) says that, after a most laborious study, Calonne was unable to submit a clear and trustworthy statement to the Assembly of Notables. " Cette assemblée n'a pas su, ou n'a pas pu démêler la vérité dans le fatras de chiffres soumis à son examen."

[1] Humbert, " Essai sur les Finances et la Comptabilité chez les Romains."

a number of sound administrative principles, which, even after a lapse of eighteen centuries, the rulers of nations have not as yet taken sufficiently to heart. He saw that low salaries and insecurity of tenure connoted corruption and misgovernment, and accordingly he gave all his provincial officials not only fixed, but high, salaries.[1] He and his immediate successors put a stop to those frequent changes of officials which did an infinite amount of harm to the Roman, as they have in our day to the Ottoman, Empire.[2] He

[1] The Proconsuls received 1,000,000 sesterces a year. The Procurators were divided into sexagenarii, centenarii, etc., according as their salaries were 60,000, 100,000, etc., sesterces (Marquardt, " L'Organisation de l'Empire Romain," vol. ii., p. 586). The first step taken by Clive, and later by Lord Cornwallis, in India to stop the abuses prevalent in their times was to raise salaries. A similar course has been followed in Egypt.

[2] "One of the secrets of the better administration of Cæsar's provinces was the length of time during which one of these Legates might be kept in a single province. Thus, in Tiberius's reign, Sabinus governed Mœsia for twenty, and Silius Gaul for seven, years, while somewhat later Galba was in Spain for eight" (Greenidge, "Roman Public Life," p. 434).

The very well-informed author of "Turkey in Europe,"

created a regular civil service, and, by imposing a limit on the ages of officials, impressed young and competent men into his service.[1] Courts for the trial of corrupt provincial Governors were instituted, and some—such as Verres of Sicilian, and Gallus of Egyptian, fame—were

---

who writes under the pseudonym of "Odysseus," says (p. 86) that so far back as the eleventh century a Vizier (Nizamu-'l-Mulk) wrote a work called "The Science of Government," in which he "recommended that provincial governors and agents should be often moved, and not allowed to become too powerful." Speaking of the period of Turkish history when the Phanariots had risen to positions of importance, he says (p. 309): "Hospodars, dragomans, and patriarchs alike bought their offices for enormous sums. . . . The Porte changed them all as often as possible, in order to increase the number of sales, but left them a free hand in the matter of filling their own pockets."

The practice of effecting frequent changes of officials has survived up to our own days in Turkey. The results which ensued from the adoption of this policy in Egypt were stated by Mr. Cave in 1876 (see "Modern Egypt," vol. i., pp. 30-31).

[1] Another wise regulation made by the Romans, but not till the time of Marcus Aurelius, and which was eventually incorporated into the Justinian Code, was that, without a special dispensation from the Emperor, no Governor was appointed to rule the province in which he was born (Gibbon, "Decline and Fall," c. xvii.).

brought to justice.[1] More than this, some rare instances may be cited of Governors who took a real interest in the well-being of the provincials. The elder Cato drove the usurers out of Sardinia, and abolished the local contributions usually paid to the prætors.[2] The very valuable correspondence, which has fortu-

[1] It is worthy of note that one of the last acts performed by the Senate (*circa* A D. 470) before the final extinction of the Western Empire was the trial and condemnation of Arvandus, a Prefect of Gaul, who had rendered himself conspicuous by his oppression of the provincials. Gregorovius ("Rome in the Middle Ages," vol. i., p. 241) says: "This trial was one of the most honourable deeds which graced the dying days of the Senate. For Gaul, however, it was but an empty and formal satisfaction, since the Governors of the province continued, not only to drain it with the same rapacity as before, but further betrayed it into the hands of the Visigoths; in fact, the immediate successor of Arvandus, Seronatus (a new Catiline), was for these offences punished by the Senate with death."

[2] "Fugatique ex insula feneratores, et sumptus, quos in cultum prætorum socii facere soliti erant, circumcisi, aut sublati" (Livy, xxxii. 27). Livy adds that, although Cato was a man of the highest integrity (sanctus et innocens), it was generally thought that he was too severe on the usurers (asperior tamen in fenore coercendo habitus). It is highly probable that Cato, with the best intentions, violated every sound economic law, and ended by doing more harm than good.

nately been preserved, between the Emperor Trajan and the younger Pliny also shows that at times a real interest in the well-being of the subject races was evinced both by the central and by the local authorities. Occasionally, also, some unusually stout-hearted official protected the provincials from the rapacity of the numerous fashionable and money-grabbing adventurers who flocked from Rome in order to prey upon them. I have a strong fellow-feeling for that Bithynian prætor whose justice has been immortalized by Catullus,[1] for I have had a somewhat wide personal experience of the race of company-mongers to which Catullus belonged, and of their angry vituperation—though in prose rather than in poetry. Occasionally, also, Governors were found too honest to take advantage of the opportunities

[1] "Huc ut venimus, incidere nobis
   Sermones varii ; in quibus, quid esset
   Iam Bithynia, quo modo se haberet,
   Ecquonam mihi profuisset ære.
   Respondi id quod erat, nihil neque ipsis
   Nunc prætoribus esse nec cohorti,
   Cur quisquam caput unctius referret,
   Præsertim quibus esset irrumator
   Prætor, nec faceret pili cohortem."
                              (Catullus, x.)

afforded to them for illicit gain. Vespasian returned from Africa no richer than when he went there.[1]

These cases were, however, quite exceptional. As a general rule, *Virtus post nummos* was the watchword of every class of Roman society—at all events, during late republican times. "The subject was regarded as existing for the empire, rather than the empire for the subject."[2] The tribute was fixed at a high figure, not merely in order to obtain money, but also with a view to crippling the resources of the conquered nation, and preventing them from renewing the struggle for independence.[3] It bore with special hardness on the subject races, because the provincial officials, being practically under no control, exacted not only the tribute, but additional contributions on their own private accounts. Varus, who

[1] "Rediit certe nihilo opulentior" (Suet., Div. Vesp., 4).
[2] Greenidge, "Roman Public Life," p. 439.
[3] "Les guerres, conduites hors de l'Italie, donnèrent lieu à des contributions, qui s'élevèrent à des sommes très considérables, et le paiement en fut reparti sur une série d'années, pour affaiblir l'ennemi pour longtemps et lui enlever son indépendance" (Marquardt, "L'Organisation Financière," vol. i., p. 232).

eventually met his death in the forests of Germany, went, a poor man, as Governor to Syria, and in two years became a millionaire.[1] The tax-gatherers and their inevitable companions, in ancient as in modern times, the usurers,[2] were let loose on the unfortunate provincials, and, as Mr. Warde Fowler says, "It is hard to say which wrought the most mischief to the Empire."[3] In B.C. 167, the

[1] Arnold, "Studies, etc.," p. 223. Another notorious case was that of Licinius, whom Augustus named Procurator of Gaul. Dion Cassius (liv. 21) says that he combined the avarice of a barbarian (he was originally a slave) with all the pretensions of a Roman (ὄυτος οὖν πλεονεξίᾳ μὲν βαρβαρικῇ, ἀξιώσει δὲ Ῥωμαϊκῇ χρώμενος, κ.τ.λ.).

[2] The usurers were, of course, very unpopular. Cato contended that there was no difference between a money-lender and a murderer, and that the former occupied a deservedly lower position in public estimation than a thief. The subject is discussed by Mommsen in his History, vol. iii., c. xii. It is interesting, in this connection, to note that the system of trusts, of which we have heard a good deal lately, was not unknown to the ancient Romans. There existed "coalitions of rival companies, in order jointly to establish monopolist prices."

[3] Warde Fowler, "Social Life at Rome, etc.," p. 94. In Ismail Pasha's time the Egyptian tax-gatherers were frequently accompanied by a staff of usurers, who bought up the crops of the cultivators in advance at prices which were ruinous to the latter (see "Modern Egypt," vol. i., p. 38).

Senate, on the occasion of sending a commission to Macedonia, expressed an opinion that the presence of the tax-farmer was incompatible with the existence of either justice or liberty.[1]

Whatever harvest there was left to reap after the corrupt officials and the rapacious publicans had done their worst, was garnered by commercial adventurers of the type of Catullus, who were backed with all the weight of the capitalist interest in Rome. Marcus Junius Brutus, who has gone down to posterity as a model of republican virtue, did not scruple, at a time when the legal rate of interest was fixed at 12 per cent., to demand 48 per cent. on a loan made to a Cypriote town, and quarrelled with the somewhat more scrupulous Cicero, because, as Governor of Cilicia, the latter placed obstacles in the way of the execution of this leonine contract.[2]

[1] "Ubi publicanus esset, ibi aut jus publicum vanum, aut libertatem sociis nullam esse" (Livy, xlv. 18).

[2] Marquardt, "Organisation de l'Empire Romain," vol. ii., p. 565. Cicero's letter to his brother Quintus, when the latter was Proprætor in Asia Minor ("Cicero's Correspondence," Tyrrell, vol. i., pp. 250-69), breathes something of the benign spirit which inspires modern Imperialism.

Cicero himself pleaded eloquently the cause of the *insanum forum*, which answered to our Stock Exchange, in a speech on the Manilian law, bearing a very close resemblance to the arguments brought forward at times in London, and still more in Paris, on behalf of the bondholders of foreign loans.[1]

It is one of the peculiarities of an administrative system which is honeycombed with corrupt practices that accusations of corruption are sown broadcast, and when, as often happens, they are false, do almost as much harm as the corrupt practices themselves.[2] This is what frequently happened in ancient times at Rome. Charges of corruption, often true, and also probably at times false, which were usually coupled with accusations of high treason, became a fertile source of wealth to the Treasury.[3] Sallust, in spite of the some-

---

[1] Warde Fowler, "Social Life, etc.," p. 75.

[2] "The Roman Emperors employed certain agents (styled *agentes in rebus*) to visit the provinces and furnish the supreme Government with information respecting their condition. . . . They are accused of having ruined persons in the remote provinces by false accusations" (Lewis, "Government of Dependencies," pp. 162-63).

[3] "Ancharius Priscus Caesium Cordum pro consule Cretae postulaverat repetundis, addito majestatis crimine, quod

what vapid moral sentiments which he has left on record, did not hesitate (B.C. 45) to use his position as Governor of Numidia in order to accumulate vast stores of wealth, which, probably owing to the fact that he was a eulogist of the Cæsarian policy, he was never made to disgorge. The gossip-loving Suetonius records that Titus, the *amor ac deliciæ generis humani*, was strongly suspected of corrupt practices—a suspicion which, however, did him more good than harm in public estimation, for the easy-going morality of the day readily condoned venality if unaccompanied by the more baneful vices exhibited by a Nero.[1]

That a vast improvement took place in the early days of the empire cannot be doubted.

---

tum omnium accusationum complementum erat" (Tacitus, Ann., iii. 38). Pliny the Younger, in his panegyric on the Emperor Trajan, says: "Locupletabant et fiscum et ærarium non tam Voconiæ et Juliæ leges, quam majestatis singulare et unicum crimen eorum qui crimine vacarent" (Pliny, In Paneg., 42).

[1] "Suspecta rapacitas, quod constabat in cognitionibus patris nundinari præmiarique solitum; denique propalam alium Neronem et opinabantur et prædicabant. At illi ea fama pro bono cessit conversaque est in maximas laudes neque vitio ullo reperto et contra virtutibus summis" (Suet., Div. Tit., c. vii.).

Mr. Ferrero, who certainly cannot be accused of the strong Cæsarian sympathies which somewhat colour the views of the great German historian Mommsen, says that from the days of Augustus " a wonderful economic prosperity began for the whole Empire."[1] It may, perhaps, be held by some that the stimulus thus given to material prosperity was dearly bought at the expense of founding a system of government which arrested the progress of Hellenism, crushed out the nascent liberties of nations, and, to use an expressive phrase of Professor Mahaffy's,[2] numbed the intellect of the world. But I venture to think that a more reasonable, more correct, and more philosophic view to take is to surmise that the *Pax Romana* was a necessary phase through which the world had to pass before those moralizing influences, which we owe mainly to the Jew and the Teuton, could be brought to bear on the destinies of mankind, and thus usher in a period when the arrested culture and humanity of the Hellene could exert their legitimate influence.

[1] Ferrero, " Greatness and Decline, etc.," vol. v., p. 338.
[2] " Greek Life and Thought," p. 617.

Great, however, as were the reforms accomplished by Augustus and some of his more immediate successors, it must be admitted that they were, for the most part, of a purely administrative character. Notably, nothing was done to remove that great blot on ancient civilization which has been justly termed by a recent scholarly writer (Mr. Paterson) "The Nemesis of Nations." The Roman conscience, less sensitive than that of the Greek,[1] was rarely troubled by any scruples on the subject of slavery.[2] It was thought the most natural

[1] "In Greece alone men's consciences were troubled by slavery, and right down through the centuries of the decadence, when the industrial slave system ruled everywhere, the philosophers never entirely ceased protesting against what seemed an inevitable wrong" (Gilbert Murray, "The Rise of the Greek Epic," p. 19). The Greek condemnation of slavery dates from very early times. See, *inter alia*, the well-known lines in Il., xvii. 522-23; also Eur., Or., 1115, and Soph., Ajax, 485-90. Zeno upheld the modern doctrine that neither purchase nor conquest can make one man the property of another. On the other hand, as is well known, Aristotle defended the institution of slavery, and it does not appear to have been expressly condemned by Plato.

[2] Seneca, however, if he did not absolutely condemn the institution of slavery, was a strong advocate of according humane treatment to slaves. In his forty-seventh letter he says: "Servi sunt? Immo homines. Servi sunt?

thing in the world to make slaves of a conquered nation.[1] The Column of Trajan, which now stands at Rome, commemorates the quasi-depopulation of Dacia.[2]

Looking, however, at the matter from a purely administrative point of view, it may be said that the reforms only produced a partial effect—a circumstance which will not surprise those who, in modern times, have had practical experience of the enormous difficulties of

---

Immo contubernales. Servi sunt? Immo homines amici," etc.

The Essenes, a small communistic sect, of whose peculiar tenets a description is given by Josephus (Bell. Jud., ii. 8), appear to have been the first community of the ancient world to entirely reject the institution of slavery both in principle and in practice.

[1] See, *inter alia*, Lampridius, Alex., Sev. Vita., c. lv.; "Provinces of the Roman Empire," vol. i., p. 223; and Ferrero, "Decline and Greatness, etc.," vol. v., p. 134.

[2] On the condition of slaves under the ancient world, and more especially on the effect produced by slavery on Roman character and institutions, see, *inter alia*, Gibbon's "Decline and Fall," c. ii. (and notes); Merivale's "History of the Romans," vol. vii., p. 603; Mommsen's "History of Rome," Bk. IV., c. xi.; and Hodgkin's "Italy and her Invaders," vol. ii., pp. 556-65. The legal aspect of the question has recently been treated in a work by Mr. W. Buckland, entitled the "Law of Slavery."

eradicating a deep-seated evil, such as corruption, which is not condemned by the society in which the evil-doers mix. Horace, with characteristic acuteness, placed his finger on the right spot when he exclaimed: *Quid leges sine moribus!* The abuses which Augustus strove manfully to combat, though greatly mitigated in intensity, still continued to exist. The harshness and oppression of republican times were rivalled, in the days of Commodus, by that Syrian Governor (Pescennius Niger), who aspired to be Emperor and lost his life in the attempt, and who, on being petitioned by the inhabitants of his province to accord some relief of taxation, brutally replied that he regretted that he could not tax the air which they breathed.[1]

If we turn to the spirit which, in the first instance at all events, animated the merchant rulers of India and their agents, we cannot find much to gratify our national pride. The methods which they adopted did not differ

[1] "Idem Palæstinis rogantibus, ut eorum censitio levaretur idcirco, quod esset gravata, respondit: 'Vos terras vestras levari censitione vultis; ego vero etiam aerem vestrum censere vellem'" (Spartianus, "Pescennii Nigri Vita," c. vii.).

very materially from those employed by the corrupt and rapacious officials of Ancient Rome. An interval of 1,700 years had not altered human nature. The British critic of the practices of the East India Company during the latter part of the eighteenth century could, without exaggeration, echo the cry of the Roman satirist of the early part of the second century :

"Quæ reverentia legum,
Quis metus aut pudor est unquam properantis avari?"[1]

We now, indeed, know that Warren Hastings was a great statesman, and that a just or correct description of the administration over which he presided is not to be gathered from the inflated if eloquent diatribes of Burke,[2] or the

[1] Juvenal, xiv. 176.
[2] I quote one, and by no means an extreme, instance. On the final day of the long trial (June 16, 1794), Burke said : " My Lords, you have seen the condition of the country when the native government was succeeded by that of Mr. Hastings; you have seen the happiness and prosperity of all its inhabitants, from those of the highest to those of the lowest rank. You have seen the very reverse of all this under the government of Mr. Hastings, the country itself, all its beauty and glory, ending in a jungle for wild beasts. You have seen flourishing families reduced to implore that pity which the poorest man and

pungent and somewhat laboured witticisms of Sheridan.[1] Nevertheless, even after making a liberal allowance for the exaggerations of rhetorical pleaders, it cannot be doubted that, at the close of the eighteenth century, the administration of India was bad, and that at a somewhat earlier period it was even worse. During the temporary absence from India of Clive (1760-65)—a period which Sir Alfred

---

the meanest situation might well call for. You have seen whole nations in the mass reduced to a condition of the same distress. These things in his government at home; abroad, scorn, contempt, and derision cast upon and covering the British name; war stirred up, and dishonourable treaties of peace made, by the total prostitution of British faith " (" Burke's Works," vol. viii., p. 438).

Mr. Rice Holmes (" History of the Indian Mutiny," p. 9), on the other hand, says: " No other than that policy (*i.e.*, the policy adopted by Warren Hastings) which Burke held up to execration would have saved the Empire in the most momentous crisis through which it has ever passed."

[1] Sheridan termed the East India Company "highwaymen in kid gloves." On October 7, 1785, he said: "Alike in the political and military line could be observed auctioneering Ambassadors and trading Generals; and thus one saw a revolution brought about by affidavits, an army employed in executing an arrest, a town besieged by a note of hand, a Prince dethroned for the balance of an account."

Lyall says " throws grave and unpardonable dishonour on the English name "[1]—many of the local officials of the East India Company, being under no effective legal or moral control, "lost all sense of honour, justice, and integrity; they plundered as Moghuls or Marathas had done before them, though in a more systematic and business-like fashion; the eager pursuit of wealth, and its easy acquisition, had blunted their consciences, and produced general insubordination." So moderate a politician as Sir George Cornewall Lewis carried the full weight of the accusation down to a later date. In the debate on the India Act of 1858 he said: " I do most confidently maintain that no civilized government ever existed on the face of this earth which was more corrupt, more perfidious, and more capricious than the East India Company was from 1758 to 1784, when it was placed under Parliamentary control." From the day when that control was established, matters greatly improved. The merchant rulers of India during their subsequent period of dominion may have made, and without doubt did make, some

[1] " British Dominion in India," p. 143.

mistakes; but the humane and statesmanlike spirit which animated their counsels is fitly represented by the noble lines written by Macaulay, and inscribed under the statue of Lord William Bentinck at Calcutta.[1]

It was not, however, until seventy-four years later that the adoption of the principle which lies at the root of all sound administration, and which in quite recent times has been flagrantly violated in Turkey, Egypt, and the Congo, was forced upon the rulers of India by the convulsion of 1857. That principle is that administration and commercial exploitation should not be entrusted to the same hands.[2] State officials may err, but they have

[1] "He abolished cruel rites; he effaced humiliating distinctions; he gave liberty to the expression of public opinion; his constant study was to elevate the intellectual and moral character of the natives committed to his charge."

[2] Although personally I hold strongly to this opinion, I should perhaps mention that it is not universally accepted Thus, a very able and competent authority (Sir Charles Lucas, Preface to Lewis's "Government of Dependencies," p. xxiv), writing in 1891, says: "On the whole, it may be said that the second birth of chartered companies is one of the most hopeful, as it is one of the most unexpected, signs of the times." Sir Charles Lucas appears to rely mainly on improved means of communication and on the force of public opinion

no interests to serve but those of good government, whereas commercial agents must almost of necessity at times neglect the welfare of the subject race in the real or presumed pecuniary interests of their employers. For the last fifty years, although errors of judgment may possibly be imputed to the rulers of India, more especially in the direction of a somewhat reckless adaptation of Western ideas to Eastern requirements, not a word of reproach can be breathed against the spirit which has animated their rule. However much those intentions may at times be challenged by the esurient youth of the day, whose mental equipoise has been upset by the institutions and training which they owe to their alien benefactors,[1] the

---

to prevent a repetition of the abuses which formerly arose under the system which he advocates. These are unquestionably considerations of weight. Nevertheless, I cannot but think that the system is radically defective and vicious; all the more so because public opinion may not improbably be largely influenced by those who are interested in the perpetuation of the abuses. This is certainly what happened in connection with the Congo.

[1] An anecdote or a chance allusion is at times, to use an expression of Bacon's, more luciferous than ponderous argument. I remember hearing such an anecdote in India. A wealthy young Bengali, who was declaiming against the

uprightness, the benevolence, and the sincerity of the rulers of India has been fully recognized by the wisest and most statesmanlike of the indigenous races.[1]

British Government, and expressing a wish that they should be expelled from India, was asked what he would do if, as the result of the anarchy and confusion which would ensue, his personal property was confiscated. "What should I do, sir?" was his reply; "I should apply to the High Court." British ideas of justice had so unconsciously penetrated into his mind that he could not conceive a condition of affairs which involved the possibility of the supremacy of the law being attainted.

[1] Sir Syud Ahmed, the founder of the College at Alighur, said: "Be not unjust to that nation which is ruling over you, and think also on this—how upright is her rule. Of such benevolence as the English Government shows to the foreign nations under her there is no example in the history of the world."

Sir Salar Jung, the late very capable Minister of the Nizam of Hyderabad, said: "The enlightened classes in India recognize that the rule of England has secured us against incessant strife, involving a perpetual exhaustion of the resources of our communities, and also that, by a just administration of equal laws, a very sufficient measure of individual liberty is now our birthright."

These are both Mohammedans. A distinguished Parsi gentleman (Sir Pherozshah Mehta) said at the National Congress of 1905: "The future of India is linked with that of England, and it is to England that India must always look for guidance, assistance, and protection in her need."

If we turn to the comparative results obtained by ancient and modern imperialists; if we ask ourselves whether the Romans, with their imperfect means of locomotion and communication, their relatively low standard of public morality, and their ignorance of many economic and political truths, which have now become axiomatic, succeeded as well as any modern people in assimilating the nations which the prowess of their arms had brought under their sway, the answer cannot be doubtful. They succeeded far better.[1] It is true that in the East they did so at the cost of losing their national individuality. In that quarter " they conquered the world only to give it to Hellas ";[2] but in the West they left

[1] Mr. Ferrero ("Character and Events, etc.," vol. i., Preface, p. v), speaking of "the struggle between the Occident and the Orient," says that it is "a problem that Rome succeeded in solving as no European civilization has since been able to do, making the countries of the Mediterranean basin share a common life in peace."

[2] Psichari ("Études de Philologie Neo-Grecque"), quoted in Arnold's "Studies of Roman Imperialism," p. 242. Professor Flint also ("History of Philosophy of History," p. 56), quoted by Laurie ("Historical Survey of Christian Education," p. 399), says: " Rome made the world Roman, and became herself cosmopolitan."

their own abiding mark on the destinies of mankind. They either Romanized the races who were at first their subjects and eventually their masters, or left those races to be the willing agents of their own Romanization.

A great deal has been said and written on the subject of the inability of modern European Powers to assimilate subject races. It is very generally held that this inability is especially marked in the case of the British.[1]

[1] Mr. Hogarth ("The Nearer East," p. 277) says, speaking of Egypt: "The French and Italians acquire more sympathy with the native society than the Briton does; they can assimilate where the latter governs." I dealt with this subject to a certain extent in my recent work on "Modern Egypt," vol. ii., pp. 235-42. I ought perhaps here to add that it is very easy to attach undue political importance to the alleged superior powers of assimilation possessed by the French in so far as those powers are proved by Egyptian evidence. In the first place, whatever sympathy exists amongst the Egyptians for the French is almost wholly based on social grounds. It would be a great mistake to suppose that it has made the Egyptians political Gallophiles. In the second place, the sympathy is very superficial. It does not extend deep down; it is confined to a small portion of the semi-Levantinized population of the towns. In the third place, the circumstances in Egypt are very peculiar. The French are not in that country in the position of Governors, but of critics of another European nation whose influence is paramount. In order to draw

That there is some truth in this statement I will not deny. Our habits are insular, and our social customs render us, in comparison at all events with the Latin races, somewhat unduly exclusive. These are characteristics which tend to create a barrier between the British and the more educated portion of the subject races, but they scarcely affect the opinions of the mass of the population. The Moslem, who, speaking about the English to Professor

---

any valid political conclusions, a comparison should be made, not between the sentiments now entertained by the Egyptians towards the French and English respectively, but between the feelings of the indigenous population of Tunis and Algiers towards the French, and those entertained by the inhabitants of India and Egypt towards the British. I am not sufficiently acquainted with Algerian or Tunisian facts to justify me in instituting any such comparison, but I have a strong conviction that the mass of the Egyptian population, if they are to be ruled by any foreigners, would greatly prefer that those foreigners should be of British rather than of any other nationality. If any change of this nature were made, I cannot help thinking that the Egyptians would soon have good reason for applying to British the remark which Thucydides (i. 76) makes about Athenian paramount power: ἄλλους γ' ἂν οὖν οἰόμεθα τὰ ἡμέτερα λαβόντας δεῖξαι ἂν μάλιστα εἴ τι μετριάζομεν. I quote later the evidence of M. Boissier and others as regards the feelings entertained by subject races towards the French in Algiers and elsewhere.

Vambéry, said, " Black is their faith, but pure and blameless is their justice,"[1] presented a phase of thought very common amongst Asiatics. Moreover, my own experience certainly leads me to the conclusion that the British generally, though they succeed less well when once the full tide of education has set in, possess in a very high degree the power of acquiring the sympathy and confidence of any primitive races with which they are brought in contact. Nothing struck me more than the manner in which young men, fresh from some British military college or university, were able to identify themselves with the interests of the wild tribes in the Soudan, and thus to govern them by sheer weight of character and without the use of force.[2]

[1] "Western Culture in Eastern Lands," p. 242.

[2] Speaking of the young men who occupy the outposts of the British Empire, a German who recently travelled in India says: "He is so ridiculously young; he has no one to speak to; any day an ambushed assassin may put a bullet into him; even shooting and riding are hardly permitted; yet he is cheerful, pleasant, always at work with or for his men; he is not only a soldier, but something of a linguist, a student as well. Undaunted by the deadly monotony, the utter loneliness, he carries his burden of responsibility courageously; and if death calls him from his task there are always others ready to take

I need not, however, dwell on this branch of the subject at any length; for, although the idiosyncrasies and the special aptitudes of the different European nations count for something, the real truth is that, in a broad general view of modern Imperialism, this aspect of the question may be regarded as a detail. So far as I know, the only European people which have shown any considerable powers of assimilation in dealing with the indigenous races of Asia and Africa, are the Greeks. Mr. Hogarth, in his work entitled "The Nearer East," says, truly enough: "The Greek excels all [others], being a Nearer Eastern himself."[1]

---

his place, unshakably confident in their country's destiny. Hard things are said at home of the English subaltern. You do not know him, you cannot judge him aright, till you have seen him on the North-West Frontier" (Review in the *Spectator* of March 6, 1909, of Count von Königsmarck's "Die Engländer in Indien").

The insufficient recognition sometimes accorded to these young men by a small section of their countrymen finds, I trust, some compensation in the high value attached to their services by those who, like myself, have seen them at work. They constitute, in my opinion, the flower of the youth of England. No other nation possesses Imperial agents to compare with them.

[1] "The Nearer East," p. 277. Mr. Hogarth goes on to say: "There is no people which so easily obtains the

The two main agencies which were employed in the Hellenization of the ancient world were commerce and culture. In respect to the former point, the Greek still preserves a certain supremacy in the East. More especially, he is a retail trader of incomparable excellence. The intellectual advance of other nationalities has, of course, destroyed the ancient Greek monopoly of culture.

No modern Imperialist nation has, however, shown powers of assimilation at all comparable to those displayed by the Romans. The untoward zeal of the Jesuit missionaries would of itself—even if no other causes had intervened—have effectually checked any effective fusion between the Spaniards and the indigenous subjects of their American colonies. " According to Dr. Livingstone, the only art the natives learnt after five hundred years' intercourse with the Portuguese was that of

---

confidence of the poorer *fellahin*, and so quickly adapts itself to Nilotic conditions." I agree about the powers of adaptation; I am not so sure about the confidence. Most of the Greeks with whom the Egyptian peasantry are brought in contact are unfortunately either money-lenders or *bakals* (drink-sellers).

distilling spirits from a gun-barrel."[1] I am not aware that the Dutch have shown any particular genius in the direction of assimilation; indeed, the relations between the Dutch settlers and the natives of South Africa would seem to point to a directly opposite conclusion.[2] The recent Belgian failure—due more to their ruler than to the Belgian nation—is notorious. Italian and American[3] Imperialism are of too recent a date to enable any conclu-

---

[1] Bosworth Smith, "Mohammed and Mohammedanism," p. 38. It ought in fairness to be added that this quotation, taken by itself, conveys a somewhat exaggerated idea of Dr. Livingstone's views. On p. 410 and elsewhere in his "Missionary Tales in South Africa" he speaks highly of the labours of the Jesuit and other Catholic missionaries in the cause of education in Portuguese Africa.

[2] From the fact that, in their Eastern colonies, the Dutch have done all in their power to discourage the acquisition of a knowledge of Dutch amongst their native subjects, I think it may be inferred not only that they have never attempted to carry out a policy of fusion, but that they are altogether opposed to making the attempt.

[3] The experiment now being made in Cuba is of the greatest interest. To occupy the country was easy. If the Government of the United States succeeds in establishing a good government in that island without a military occupation, they will afford to the world a novel and very remarkable object-lesson in the execution of an Imperial policy.

## ANCIENT AND MODERN IMPERIALISM 79

sion to be drawn as to their results. The same may be said of German Imperialism.

There remain Russia, France, and England.

A very general idea prevails that the Russians possess special powers of assimilation with subject races. Lack of evidence renders it difficult for anyone who has not visited the Asiatic provinces of Russia to form a matured opinion on this subject. It is, however, a fact that a few Asiatics, such as Loris Melikoff, who was an Armenian, and Alikhanoff, who was a Lesghian from the Caucasus and a Moslem, have risen to posts of considerable distinction in the Russian service. Moreover, in their social relations, the Russians cannot be accused of being exclusive. They are certainly much less so than the British. Mr. Schuyler, who visited Turkestan in 1876, said: "The natives held aloof from the Russians, rather than the Russians from the natives."[1] On

[1] Schuyler, "Turkestan," vol. ii., p. 233.

Very insufficient attention is, I think, paid to this aspect of the question. It is often assumed by those whose acquaintance with Eastern society is somewhat superficial that the absence of close social intercourse between Europeans and Easterns is wholly due to the attitude of the former. Such is very far from being the case. I have

the other hand, these advantages are more than counterbalanced by great defects. Whatever may be the case now, there can be no doubt that at one time the Russian administration in Central Asia was extremely bad. The worst officers in the army were sent to Turkestan, which was regarded " as a refuge for the scum of military society."[1] A Commission composed of Russian officials reported: " We have not been able to inspire the natives with confidence. . . . The high moral qualities which ought to have carried the civilizing mission of the Russians to the natives have been wanting."[2]

---

known numerous cases in which the action of Easterns who were disposed to live on terms of intimate friendship with Europeans, who spoke their language fluently and who were very sympathetically inclined towards them, was strongly resented by their own countrymen and co-religionists.

According to the well-known historian, Jabarti, when the French evacuated Egypt at the close of the eighteenth century, the Turks and the leading Egyptian Ulema caused all the Moslems—male and female—who had lived on good terms with the French to be executed, not on account of political hatred, but because it was held that they had become polluted by the association.

[1] Schuyler, "Turkestan," vol. ii., p. 220.
[2] *Ibid.*, p. 225.

## ANCIENT AND MODERN IMPERIALISM

The latest and most competent witness on this subject is Professor Vambéry. He has visited Central Asia—that "den of Asiatic barbarism and ferocity,"[1] as he calls it. He fully recognizes the improvements made by the Russians; but he adds that "in order to work successfully, the Russians must make themselves more familiar with the language, religion, customs, history, and characteristics of the natives, and have a more intimate intercourse with them than has been the case hitherto."[2] He scouts the idea that the Russians possess any special aptitude for assimilation, and, although I am aware that he is regarded by the Russians themselves as a prejudiced witness, I see no reason to doubt the general accuracy of his conclusions. Differences of religion bar the way to intermarriage, and without intermarriage there can be no social equality or real fusion, any more than without a knowledge of the vernacular language there can be any intimate social intercourse.[3]

[1] "Western Culture, etc.," p. 119.
[2] *Ibid.*, p. 78.
[3] "Very few Russian officials are acquainted with the native tongue, and those who know it will not use it, for

I turn to the case of the French. Has the genius of the most quick-witted and cosmopolitan nation in Europe been able to solve the problem? Apparently not. Some trifling successes may, as in the case of Egypt, have been gained, but there has been no real assimilation, no effective fusion of the Western and of the Eastern races. A high authority (M. Boissier) speaks very decidedly on this subject. After paying a well-deserved tribute to the material progress effected under French auspices in Algeria, he goes on to say that, in one respect, the policy of his countrymen has been a complete failure. They have not gained the sympathies of the natives. There has been nothing approaching to a fusion. The two

---

fear of losing the respect of the natives, who might explain the foreigner's use of the native tongue as a sign that he wants to ingratiate himself with them and court their favour" (*Ibid.*, pp. 70, 71).

Sir Donald Mackenzie Wallace, who speaks with high authority on all matters connected with Russia, writes: "If we compare a Finnish village in any stage of Russification with a Tartar village, of which the inhabitants are Mohammedans, we cannot fail to be struck by the contrast. In the latter, though there may be many Russians, there is no blending of the two races. Between them religion has raised an impassable barrier" ("Russia," vol. i., p. 198).

## ANCIENT AND MODERN IMPERIALISM

races live in different and even hostile camps.[1] The Romans, he thinks, succeeded better.[2]

[1] "Mais il faut reconnaître aussi que notre succès n'est pas entier. Dans une partie de notre tâche, qui n'était pas la moindre, nous avons tout à fait échoué. Après avoir vaincu les anciens habitants, nous n'avons pas su les gagner. Aucune fusion, aucun rapprochement ne s'est fait entre eux et nous; ils vivent à part, gardant fidèlement leurs croyances, leurs habitudes, et, ce qui est plus dangereux, leurs haines. Ils profitent des avantages que notre domination leur procure sans nous en être reconnaissants. L'Algérie contient deux populations voisines et séparées, qui ne se disputent plus, qui paraissent même se supporter, mais qui au fond sont mortellement ennemies l'une de l'autre, et qu'on n'imagine pas devoir jamais se confondre. C'est une situation grave, qui rend notre autorité précaire, et donne beaucoup à réfléchir aux esprits sages et prévoyants" (Boissier, "L'Afrique Romaine," pp. 315-16).

*Le Temps*, in its issue of August 28, 1909, quotes a letter recently written by an educated and apparently Francophile Annamite to M. Le Myre de Vilers, ex-Governor-General of Cochin China, in which the following passages occur: "Il est triste de dire que la majorité des Annamites n'est pas francophile: ce n'est pas qu'ils aient des motifs sérieux de se plaindre, mais ils n'aiment pas le Français uniquement parcequ'il est Français. ... Les Annamites parlant et écrivant le Français ne sont pas forcément les amis de la France."

[2] "De ce qu'on vient de voir il résulte que les Romains avaient mieux réussi que nous dans la conquête des indigènes" (Boissier, "L'Afrique Romaine," p. 354).

Lastly, how does the matter stand as regards ourselves? We have endeavoured to be as elastic as the somewhat cast-iron dogmas of Western civilization admit. Speaking from my own experience, I should say that the absence of that social adaptability, in which the French excel, is to some extent compensated in the case of the English by a relatively

---

On September 5 the same newspaper published a letter from a correspondent (Lieutenant-Colonel Bernard), who is evidently well acquainted with his subject, in which he says: "Sans doute il règne dans certains milieux un optimisme officiel et l'on proclame, en toute occasion, que la France se distingue des autres nations colonisatrices par les sentiments d'affection qu'elle sait inspirer à tous ses sujets. On oppose notre humeur bienveillante, notre familiarité facile et gaie à la raideur et à la dignité des Anglais et des Hollandais. Nos voisins savent se faire craindre, ils peuvent se faire estimer; notre lot est meilleur, et sans efforts nous nous faisons aimer. Ce sont là des lieux communs qui satisfont notre vanité, mais que toutes les observations sincères démentent. Dans les colonies, nous sommes pour l'indigène l'étranger et le maître, et cela suffit pour éveiller l'antipathie et susciter la haine."

It is as well that the truth should be boldly stated. Both in France and England ignorance of the real facts in connection with this subject, and national pride, are apt to mislead public opinion and to obscure the true issue.

high degree of administrative and political elasticity.[1] Save in dealing with some exceptionally barbarous practice, such as Sati,[2] we have followed the example of Rome in respecting local customs. Indeed, it may be doubted whether we have not gone too far in this direction, for we have often stereotyped bad customs, and allowed them to assume the

[1] The French are the inheritors of the principles of the Revolution, and those principles, as Mr. Fisher very truly remarks ("Napoleonic Statesmanship, Germany," p. 374), were the legacy of eighteenth-century philosophy, "which took little heed of the various temperaments and idiosyncrasies of men and nations, regarding humanity as something homogeneous through place and time, capable of being nourished by the same food and rescued by the same medicines. It paid scant attention to historical conditions, believing that in politics, as in physics, there was a mathematical art of discovery and scientific truth." Orientals, when they are reformers, suffer from the same defect, but in a far higher degree. Nubar Pasha was quite right to introduce the French code into Egypt, but he did not take nearly sufficient care to modify either the substantive law or the procedure to meet the special requirements of his adopted country.

[2] It is worthy of remark that the Doseh festival, with all its savage practices, which used to be held in Egypt, was not suppressed by the English, but by the Khedive (Tewfik Pasha) on his own initiative, before the British occupation took place.

force of law.[1] We have not interfered seriously with the practice of infant marriages. Save in respect to slavery,[2] we have left intact the personal law both of Hindoos and Mohammedans—albeit that in both cases the codes were drawn up centuries ago to suit the conditions of primitive societies. But in spite of these, and other illustrations of a like nature which might be cited, do not let us for one moment imagine that we have not been innovators, and, in the eyes of the ordinary conservative

[1] "Usage, once recorded upon evidence given, immediately becomes written and fixed law. Nor is it any longer obeyed as usage.... There would be little evil in the British Government giving to native custom a constraining force which it never had in purely native society, if popular opinion could be brought to approve of the gradual amelioration of that custom. Unfortunately for us, we have created the sense of legal right before we have created a proportionate power of distinguishing good from evil in the law upon which the legal right depends (Maine, "Village Communities," pp. 72, 73).

[2] In 1843, an Act was passed by the Indian Legislature which provided that the status of slavery should not be recognized by any law-court in the country, criminal or civil. No such sweeping reform has been effected in Egypt, but a series of measures have been adopted, the general result of which is that the institution of slavery is moribund (see "Modern Egypt," vol. ii., pp. 495-504).

Eastern, rash innovators. Freedom of contract, the principle of *caveat emptor*, rigid fixity of fiscal demands, the expropriation of land for non-payment of rent,[1] even the commonplace Western idea that a man must be proved to be guilty of an offence before he can be punished,[2] are almost as great innovations as the principle of representation accompanied by all the electoral paraphernalia of Europe. These divergent habits of thought on economic, juridical, and administrative questions have served to enhance the strength of the very

[1] I do not know how the matter stood in the days of the Republic, but I find in my Commonplace Book a note to the effect that Ulpian, who was killed in A.D. 228, laid down in his digest that " it was the rule of Roman law in contracts for rent that a tenant was not bound to pay if any *vis major* prevented him from reaping."

[2] Not long ago certain districts in the Algerian Hinterland, where military law used to be applied, were brought under the operation of the ordinary codes. The comment of one of the principal Algerian Sheikhs on this change was as follows : " Then," he said, " there will be no justice ; witnesses will be required." He was not in the least struck with the fact that in the absence of witnesses an innocent man might possibly be condemned. What struck him was that, as no one could be condemned without witnesses, many guilty people would escape punishment (Parliamentary Paper, Egypt, No. 1 of 1907, p. 85).

formidable and elemental forces, such as differences of religion, of colour, and of social habits, which are ever tending to sunder the governing race from that which is governed. There has been no thorough fusion, no real assimilation between the British and their alien subjects, and, so far as we can now predict, the future will in this respect be but a repetition of the past.[1] *Fata obstant.* The foundations on which the barrier wall of separation is built may be, and, without doubt, to a certain extent are, the result of prejudice rather than of reason; but however little we may like to recognize the fact, they are of so solid a character, they appeal so strongly to instincts and sentiments which lie deep down in the hearts of men and women, that for generations to come they will probably defy whatever puny, albeit well-intentioned, efforts may be made to undermine them.

[1] The policy of fusion between the British and Dutch races in South Africa is now being tried under circumstances which, I would fain hope, afford good promise of success. The measures recently adopted with a view to the execution of this policy appear to me to be eminently wise and statesmanlike. Of course, the problem presents itself for solution in South Africa under conditions widely differing from those which obtain in India or Egypt.

From this point of view, therefore, British Imperialism has, in so far as the indigenous races of Asia and Africa are concerned, been a failure. But we need not lay our want of success too deeply to heart. We need not, in a fit of very uncalled-for national depreciation, think that we have failed where others might, and probably would, have succeeded. The very contrary is the case. We have failed, not because we are Englishmen, Scotchmen, or Irishmen, but because we are Westerns. We have failed because the conditions of the problem are such as to render any marked success impossible. No other modern European nation has, in any substantial degree, been more successful than ourselves,[1] and, more-

[1] M. Morand, the Director of the School of Law at Algiers, says ("De L'Importance de L'Islamisme pour la Colonisation Européenne," pp. 23-26): "La politique de la France qui, pendant de longues années, en Algérie, a été une politique d'assimilation, semble bien avoir été sans résultat.... Plus les indigènes musulmans nous connaissent et mieux ils nous connaissent, plus ils s'éloignent de nous, et les efforts faits par la France pour les faire participer aux bienfaits de la civilisation ne semblent pas avoir été récompensés.... Ceux à qui nous avons donné l'instruction, n'ont vu que les mauvais côtés de nos institutions et n'ont été frappés, dans le spectacle de notre civilisa-

over, no other European nation has ever had to deal with the problem of assimilation under difficulties at all comparable to those which the British have had to encounter in India. The Asiatic and African subjects of France and Russia are Moslems. Five-sixths of the population of India are Hindoos, and the remaining sixth are Mohammedans who have adopted that portion of the Hindoo caste system which elevates association in the act of eating and drinking to the dignity of a religious practice. Thus a very formidable barrier to unrestrained intercourse exists in India, which

---

tion, que par les vices qu'elle entraîne. Aussi, la croyance qu'ils avaient déjá dans la supériorité de leur foi, s'en est-elle accrue. 'À voir,' dit, par example, Mohammed Ben Rahal, ' les ravages que cause chez l'européen la dissolution de la famille, la dépravation des mœurs, l'alcoolisme, le malthusianisme, l'agiotage, le surmenage, l'anarchie, l'amour effréné des richesses, les amusements formidables, les jouissances immodérées, une liberté licencieuse, on en arrive à se demander qui est le plus malade des deux, et si l'Islamisme ne serait pas pour lui un refuge et une branche de salut. Qui sait s'il pourra resister autant que le musulman, n'ayant pas, comme lui, le soutien inébranlable et indestructible de la Foi.' Aussi, M. Doutté, constate-t-il que ' les musulmans instruits sont ceux qui sont le plus éloignés de nous.' "

is unknown in countries whose people hold to a less socially exclusive creed.

The comparative success of the Romans is easily explained. Their task was far more easy than that of any modern Imperial nation.

In one of those bold and profound generalizations on Eastern politics in which he excels, Sir Alfred Lyall has very truly pointed out that the Romans only had, for the most part, to deal with tribes. It was Christianity and its offshoot, Islam, that created nations and introduced the religious element into politics.[1] Now, in the process of assimilation the Romans easily surmounted any difficulties based on religion. The easy-going polytheism and pantheism of the ancient world readily adapted itself to changed circumstances. The Syrian god Bel was transformed into Zeus Belos. The Phœnician goddess Tanit became a *Dea Cœlestis* in the person of Juno, Venus, or Minerva. Her companion Baal-Hammon became Saturnus, with the Imperial epithet

[1] "It was the advent of two great militant and propagating faiths—first Christianity, next Islam—that first made religion a vital element in politics, and afterwards made a common creed the bond of union for great masses of mankind" (Lyall, "Race and Religion," p. 14).

of Augustus tacked on to his name.[1] The anomalous spectacle was presented of a Roman General returning thanks to the local gods for permitting him to gain a victory over the devotees who had trusted to their aid in order to avert defeat.[2] Alexander Severus wished to erect a temple to Christ on the Capitol of Rome, and Hadrian scattered places of worship to "unknown gods" broadcast through his wide dominions.[3] Thus religion, far from hindering, aided the work of assimilation.

[1] Similarly, when Cortes invited the Aztecs of Mexico to become Christians, "they replied they had no doubt that the God of the Christians must be a good and a great God, and as such they were willing to give him a place among the divinities of Tlascala. The polytheistic system of the Indians, like that of the ancient Greeks, was of that accommodating kind which could admit within its elastic folds the deities of any other religion without violence to itself (Prescott's "Conquest of Mexico," vol. i., p. 391).

[2] "Il est assez curieux de voir un gouverneur de la province qui a vaincu une tribu rebelle du pays et fait sur elle une riche razzia, en remercier les dieux Maures ; c'est-à-dire, les dieux mêmes des gens qu'il vient de vaincre" ("L'Afrique Romaine," p. 328).

[3] "Christo templum facere voluit, cumque inter deos recipere, quod et Hadrianus cogitasse fertur, qui templa in omnibus civitatibus sine simulacris jusserat fieri" (Lampridius, Alex. Sev. Vita., c. xliii.).

It appears also (*Ibid.*, xxix.) that Alexander Severus had

## ANCIENT AND MODERN IMPERIALISM 93

Far different has been the situation in more modern times. Alone amongst Imperialist nations, the Spaniards endeavoured to force their faith on their reluctant subjects, with results that contributed to their own undoing. In all other cases there has been toleration, but no proselytism—or, at all events, no official proselytism. That toleration has, indeed, been at times pushed so far—as in the case of the tacit acquiescence at one time accorded to the savage rites of Juggernauth—as to strain the consciences of many earnest Christians. Toleration, however, is, from a political point of view, but a poor substitute for identification. It does not tend to break down one of the most formidable obstacles which stand in the way of fusion.[1]

It is especially worthy of note that in the only case in which the Romans were brought in contact with an unassimilative religion, their

---

images of Apollonius, Christ, Abraham, Orpheus, " et hujusmodi ceteros " in his *Lararium*. All this is quite logical. Once admit polytheism, and no rational limit can be imposed on the admission of gods into the Pantheon.

[1] " C'est la religion qui divise le plus ; c'est ce qui fait aujourd'hui des indigènes nos mortels ennemis ' (" L'Afrique Romaine," p. 326).

94 ANCIENT AND MODERN IMPERIALISM

failure was complete. The stubborn Jew who demurred to paying tribute to Cæsar, not because the amount was excessive, but because the act of payment was godless, was not to be conciliated because, by the command of the Emperor Augustus, "the smoke of the sacrifice of a bullock and two lambs rose daily in their national sanctuary to the 'supreme God,'" or because, in deference to Jewish iconoclastic sentiments, the Roman soldiers, when on service at Jerusalem, were ordered to lay aside their standards, on which the effigies of the Emperors were inscribed.[1] Neither was the spirit of the Jew to be broken when the semi-insane Caligula ordered the abolition of the Sabbath and gave directions that his own statue was to be set up in the Temple at Jerusalem—an order which was subsequently rescinded in a drunken fit of lenity.[2] Conciliation

[1] "Provinces of the Roman Empire," vol. ii., p. 189.
[2] "In the year 39 the Governor of Syria, Publius Petronius, received orders from the Emperor to march with his legions into Jerusalem, and set up in the temple the statue of the Emperor. The Governor, an honourable official of the school of Tiberius, was alarmed; Jews from all the land, men and women, grey-haired, and children, flocked to him—first to Ptolemais in Syria, then to Tiberia

## ANCIENT AND MODERN IMPERIALISM 95

and cruelty, tolerance, even extending to a recognition of the God of the Jews, and brutal intolerance, proved equally in vain. In this case the Romans had to deal with a modern problem. They succeeded no better than modern Imperialists. The Jews were vanquished and dispersed, but they were never assimilated.[1]

Religion is not the sole obstacle which now prevents the operation of that most potent of assimilating influences, intermarriage. Antipathy based on colour also bars the way. The Romans had no such difficulty to encounter.[2] M. Boissier gives some curious

---

in Galilee—to entreat his mediation that the outrage might not take place. The fields throughout the country were not tilled, and the desperate multitudes declared that they would rather suffer death by the sword or famine than be willing to look on at this abomination" (*Ibid.*, vol. ii., p. 194). Vespasian and his successors reverted to the more tolerant policy of Augustus.

[1] Although the Jews were never Romanized, they did, at an earlier period of their history, fall to a certain very limited extent under Hellenic influences. See on this subject "The House of Seleucus," vol. ii., c. xxx.

[2] " Nothing contributed more to the fusion of the races and nationalities that composed the Roman Empire than the absence of any physical and conspicuous distinctions

examples based on the ancient epitaphs found in Numidia to show that intermarriage was not uncommon. Thus one Musac, manifestly a Phœnician, had a son who took the Roman name of Saturninus, and married a Roman lady, Flavia Fortunata. In the next generation the Romanization was complete. The son was called Flavius Fortunatus.[1] Such cases are now of extremely rare occurrence in countries where races of different colour and religion are brought in contact with each other. It is natural that they should be so, for, apart from other reasons, the European woman will generally resent union with the Eastern man,

---

between those races, just as nothing did more to mitigate the horrors of slavery than the fact that the slave was usually of a tint and type of features not markedly unlike those of his master" (Bryce, "Studies, etc.," vol. i., p. 65).

Martial (xi. 53) thus sang the praises of a young blue-eyed British beauty who married a Roman:

"Claudia cæruleis cum sit Rufina Britannis
Edita, quam Latiæ pectora gentis habet!
Quale decus formæ! Romanam credere matres
Italides possunt, Atthides esse suam."

[1] "L'Afrique Romaine," p. 336. Sir William Ramsay has been kind enough to furnish me with evidence of a similar character to that adduced by M. Boissier, based on Phrygian inscriptions.

who is polygamous, whilst the seclusion of women in the East offers an almost insuperable obstacle to the counter-case of the European man being attracted by the Eastern woman.[1]

There were practically only two languages in use in the ancient world—Greek and Latin. Greek held its own in the East. In the West it was the language of philosophy, and, to a certain extent, penetrated, as an instrument of general use, into the upper ranks of society. Suetonius gives a letter from Augustus to Livia which is a curious jumble of Greek and Latin.[2] In the West there was no need for Rome to impose her language on those whom she had conquered. The inhabitants of Gaul and Spain spontaneously adopted this special form of Romanization. They were eager to learn Latin, and to cast aside their barbaric names.[3] When Augustus visited Gaul twenty-

[1] The question of intermarriage is more fully treated in an appendix to this essay.

[2] Div. Claud., c. vii. See also Horace's well-known satire, Book I., x., in which he speaks of Lucilius mixing up Greek and Latin words. The earliest Roman historians wrote in Greek.

[3] It may be said that, to a certain extent, language "follows the flag." The rapidity with which Latin gained

five years after the defeat of Vercingetorix at Alesia, he found that numerous members of

ground in Gaul may be contrasted with its slow advance in Italy at an earlier period of history, before Roman Imperialism had been born. Speaking of the substitution of Latin in the place of the old Italian dialects, Mr. Wight Duff ("A Literary History of Rome," pp. 20, 21) says: "The victory of the language followed far in the wake of the victory of the State. . . . To judge from the ephemeral *graffiti* on the walls, Oscan lasted right up to the destruction of Pompeii by the eruption of A.D. 79."

Similarly, it was not until the fall of the Empire that the growth of the separate Romance languages, which eventually took the place of Latin, was unchecked (*Ibid.*, p. 25). Sir George Lewis ("Essay on the Romance Languages," p. 20) says that the Latin language was "spread by conquest," and was also "destroyed by conquest." Even after the Western Empire had been overrun by the Teutonic races, Latin died a very slow death. It survived for many centuries, notably in Italy—at all events, in so far as the educated classes were concerned. Mr. Symonds ("The Revival of Learning," p. 325) says: "The necessity felt soon after Dante's death for translating the 'Divine Comedy' into Latin sufficiently proves that a Latin poem gained a larger audience than the masterpiece of Italian literature." Petrarch regretted the decadence of Latin as a living language, and refused to read the Decameron because it was written in the vulgar tongue, on which Lord Acton remarks with great truth ("Lectures on Modern History," p. 74): "The mediæval eclipse came not from the loss of elegant Latin, but from the loss of Greek."

the Gallic nobility already bore the name of Caius Julius.[1] The younger generation, which had not witnessed or but dimly remembered the great national struggle, was becoming Romanized.[2] Less than a century later " the deliverance of the Celtic nation from the yoke of the foreigners was no longer possible, because there was no longer such a nation. The Roman yoke might be felt, according to circumstances, as a yoke, but no longer as a foreign rule."[3] It cannot be doubted that the use of the Imperial language materially aided the work of Imperial assimilation, for Latin was not merely used by scholars and by men

---

[1] Much the same thing happened in Numidia, though in that quarter the effect was less abiding. M. Boissier says (" L'Afrique Romaine," p. 338), speaking of the inscriptions on the ancient tombs: " Les plus audacieux se créèrent un nom de toutes pièces et l'empruntèrent très souvent aux plus illustres maisons de Rome; nulle part on n'a trouvé dans les inscriptions autant de Julii, de Cornelii, d'Aemilii, de Claudii, etc. Il n'est pas possible d'imaginer que ce soient tous les descendants ou des alliés de ces nobles familles." He cites one case in which a certain Q. Postumius Celsus is described as *filius Iudchadis*, manifestly a Carthaginian name.

[2] "Greatness and Decline, etc.," vol. iv., p. 176.

[3] "The Provinces of the Roman Empire," vol. i., p. 83.

of high education. It soon became the language of the people.[1]

Modern Imperialist nations have sought to use the spread of their language in order to draw political sympathy to themselves. This has been notably the case as regards the French in the basin of the Mediterranean,[2] and—

[1] M. Boissier ("L'Afrique Romaine," p. 343) gives inscriptions which show the process of Latinization in its growth, and very justly points to their bad Latinity as a proof of the general use of the language. "Naturellement le Latin de ces pauvres gens est souvent un très pauvre Latin.... Les improprietés de termes, les erreurs de grammaire, les solécismes et les barbarismes, qu'on y rencontre presque à chaque ligne, nous montrent que nous avons affaire à des ignorants, qu'ils parlent mal le Latin, mais au moins ils le parlent. Ce n'est donc pas simplement une langue d'école et d'apparat, dont quelques pédants se servent par vanité ; c'est une langue d'usage, et, comme toutes celles qui sont vivantes, elle s'approprie aux gens qui l'emploient et change avec leur dégré de culture."

[2] M. Leroy Beaulieu, speaking of Algeria, says: "L'objet de nos efforts ce doit être l'extension de l'enseignement Arabe-Français ; c'est par lui que nous prenons presque au berceau possession des générations nouvelles" ("La Colonisation," vol. i., p. 468).

French has for many years past been supplanting the use of Italian as a *lingua franca* in the Levant. It will probably for a long time to come retain its predominance as a common language in that region, just as English will though perhaps less designedly—as regards the English in India. I do not think that either nation is likely to attain any great measure of success in this direction. They will certainly be much less successful than the Romans. Neither in French, British, nor, I think I may add, Russian possessions is there the least probability that the foreign will eventually supplant the vernacular languages. In India, only 90 men and 10 women in every 10,000 of each sex read and write English.[1] There does not appear the least prospect of French

---

maintain its paramount position on the farther side of the Isthmus of Suez.

[1] "Indian Census," p. 173. It cannot, however, be doubted that of late years the number of the upper—and notably the official—classes in India who speak English has greatly increased, with the result—which is an unmixed evil—that there is less necessity than heretofore for the British officials to acquire proficiency in the vernacular languages; hence there arises a most unfortunate tendency to widen still further the breach between the rulers and the ruled. See on this subject the recent report of the committee to consider the organization of Oriental studies in London, over which Lord Reay presided (Cd. 4560), and the debate which took place in the House of Lords on September 27, 1909—notably Lord Curzon's speech, in which special allusion is made to this point.

supplanting Arabic in Algeria.[1] In direct opposition to the case of the Romans, who had to deal with conquered races eagerly desirous of adopting the language of their conquerors, modern Imperialist nations have to deal with national sentiments which often cluster round the idea that the extrusion of the vernacular language should be stoutly resisted.[2] This is what is now happening in Egypt, where the curious anomaly is presented that the Nationalist party put forward the perfectly reasonable demand that superior education should, so far as is possible, be imparted in Arabic, whilst at the same time the whole weight of British influence has had to be

[1] See "La Colonisation," vol. i., p. 467, *et seq.* As regards Tunis, M. Leroy Beaulieu (vol. ii., pp. 74, 75) says: "Les Arabes Tunisiens ont l'esprit plus délié, plus ouvert que leurs frères d'Algérie. . . . Les jeunes gens des écoles recherchent les occasions d'apprendre le Français et suivent avec zèle les cours de notre langue qu'on leur fait le soir par surcroît."

[2] A singular application of this rule is the demand—perhaps somewhat artificially created—that an attempt should be made to revive Erse in Ireland. National sentiment in Scotland has never identified itself with the preservation of Gaelic; but that, I conceive, is because Scotch nationalism, in the wider signification of the term, has become British.

brought to bear in order to prevent English being taught in the elementary schools.[1] The British Government would have been very unwise had they attempted to resist the teaching of Dutch in South Africa. As they have not done so, the language will not improbably in course of time die a natural death.[2]

[1] It cannot be too clearly understood by all who take a special interest in this subject that the demand of parents in countries such as Egypt to have their children taught some foreign language is altogether dissociated from political ideas or sympathies. It is wholly based upon conjectures, which are often erroneous, as to what particular tuition is likely to pay best.

In the early days of the British occupation of Egypt, when the question of the ultimate ascendancy of France or England was still in doubt, the number of pupils who elected to learn respectively French or English varied in direct proportion to the opinions currently entertained on this subject. The proportion had nothing whatever to do with political sympathies for either France or England. I was constantly pressed by some of the more zealous of my own countrymen to take steps with a view to discouraging French education, and steadily refused to yield to their solicitations. At present many more pupils learn English than French, because it is thought that English ascendancy is secured, and that, therefore, a knowledge of English will be more useful than that of French.

[2] Towards the close of the eighteenth century the Emperor Joseph II. attempted to enforce the exclusive use of the German language on the schools and Courts of Justice in Hungary. The failure of this policy was complete.

The importance of this question is not, however, altogether to be measured by the number of individuals who learn the foreign tongue. A further point has to be considered. With what object do the educated classes amongst the subject races acquire the linguistic knowledge? To what uses do they turn it when it is acquired?

The stimulus, whether in ancient or modern times, has manifestly been self-interest. The Gaul and the Spaniard wished to rise to high positions in the service of Rome, and before they had been Romanized for long, they were able to do so. The native of India is even now complaining in shrill tones, and, in some cases, not without a certain amount of reason, that the opportunities accorded to him for rising are insufficient. But when we turn from the original motives which impelled the ancient and the modern respectively to acquire the linguistic knowledge, to the use to which it is applied when acquired, the analogy ceases. Rather may it be said that there is a remarkable contrast; for the knowledge of Latin did not serve as a solvent. On the contrary, it knit the subject race to its conquerors, and if it eventually helped to invert the parts which had

## ANCIENT AND MODERN IMPERIALISM 105

heretofore been played, the result was due to a variety of causes, and not to any wish to subvert that Empire in which the Romanized provincial took no less pride than the true Roman. Can the same be said of any of the Asiatic or African races who, being the subjects of modern European Powers, have learnt the language of their rulers? I fear not. The bond of a common, if on one side acquired, language is, in fact, much too brittle to resist such powerful dissolvent forces as differences of religion and colour, which are constantly acting in the direction of disunion.[1] I have already alluded to the sentiments entertained by the natives of Algeria and Cochin China towards the French. In Central Asia, the first feeling of relief at the displacement by the Russians of the cruel and corrupt government of former times speedily gave way to "a general feeling of discontent. The natives began to show a preference for Mohammedan rule."[2] The case of India is

[1] "The use of a common language is consistent with the existence of the strongest antipathies between different communities" (Lewis's "Government of Dependencies," p. 269).

[2] This statement of Mr. Schuyler is quoted, and not denied, by the Russian Terentyeff ("Russia and England in Central Asia," vol. ii., p. 204).

especially strong. Here, of a truth, we have—to use a metaphor which Byron borrowed from a Greek source—been sedulously nursing the pinion which is impelling the steel into our own breasts. For more than half a century we have, perhaps unavoidably, been teaching English through the medium of English literature, and that literature, in so far as it is historical, may easily be perverted from a disquisition on the advantages of steady progress achieved by a law-abiding nation into one which eulogizes disrespect for authority, and urges on the governed the sacred duty of throwing off the yoke of unpalatable Governors. Neither, of a surety, if we—or the French in Algeria or Tunis—turn to the history of the other great Western nation, is any corrective to be found. Can we be surprised if we reap the harvest which we have ourselves sown?

My own experience in this matter confirms the conclusion to be derived from evidence of a more general nature. That conclusion is that the great proficiency in some European language often acquired by individuals amongst the subject races of the modern Imperial

## ANCIENT AND MODERN IMPERIALISM 107

Powers in no way tends to inspire political sympathy with the people to whom that language is their mother tongue. Language is not, and never can be, as in the case of Ancient Rome, an important factor in the execution of a policy of fusion. Indeed, in some ways, it rather tends to disruption, inasmuch as it furnishes the subject races with a very powerful arm against their alien rulers.[1] The writers in the *Indian Sociologist* who advocate political assassination possess considerable facility of expression in a style of English which is somewhat turgid and bombastic. The defence put forward at the trial of the wretched youth who, but recently, murdered Sir Curzon Wyllie, was composed in English, and was not wanting in eloquence.[2]

[1] " Hitherto the spread of education among the Tartars has tended rather to imbue them with fanaticism. If we remember that theological education always produces intolerance, and that Tartar education is almost exclusively theological, we shall not be surprised to find that a Tartar's religious fanaticism is generally in direct proportion to the amount of his intellectual culture " (Wallace, " Russia," vol. i., p. 204).

[2] I do not know whether Dhingra wrote his own defence, or whether it was composed for him. The most pitiful and politically noteworthy part of the document is

## 108 ANCIENT AND MODERN IMPERIALISM

I turn to another point which does not bear directly on the question of fusion, but which is highly worthy of note in any consideration of the difficulties which lie in the path of the modern, as compared to the ancient, Imperialist. I have already mentioned that, as in the case of the suppression of Druidical practices, a few faint traces of the modern spirit of humanitarianism are to be found in Roman historical records. For instance, when provincial towns or districts were devastated by some natural visitation, such as a disastrous earthquake, or an epidemic disease, relief was afforded to them, and they were temporarily exempted from the payment of tribute.[1] Again, at a much later period

---

that its author, whoever he may have been, probably believed that the wild statements he made were true.

[1] " Eodem anno duodecim celebres Asiæ urbes conlapsæ nocturno motu terræ. . . . Asperrima in Sardianos lues plurimum in eosdem misericordiæ traxit; nam centies sestertium pollicitus Cæsar, et quantum ærario aut fisco pendebant in quinquennium remisit. Magnetes a Sipylo proximi damno ac remedio habiti. Temnios, Philadelphenos, Aegeatas, Apollonidenses, quique Mosteni aut Macedones Hyrcani vocantur, et Hierocæsariam, Myrinam, Cymen, Tmolum levari idem in tempus tributis mittique

## ANCIENT AND MODERN IMPERIALISM 109

(A.D. 331), Constantine afforded generous relief to the famine-stricken people of Antioch; but it must be borne in mind that by that time Christian humanitarianism had become an active force. Moreover, indignation—whether excited by the humanizing influence of the Stoic philosophy or by other less laudable impulses—was at times displayed against the excesses of the provincial Governors.[1] But in spite of these occasional, and, in pagan days, not very convincing, humanitarian symptoms, nothing approaching to the modern "ethical process,"[2] as it has been termed by Professor

---

ex senatu placuit qui præsentia spectaret refoveretque" (Tacitus, Ann., ii. 47).

[1] "The citizens (of Rome) were indignant that their subjects should be treated as Gallus had dealt with the Egyptians. . . . Under pretext of zeal for justice and honesty, the public was venting upon the unhappy Gallus that suppressed hatred which the civil wars had left behind. . . . The large fortunes made in Egypt after the conquest were especially obnoxious to every class. Cornelius Gallus, who had made a fortune in Egypt, was destined to become the victim of all who had not enjoyed his opportunities" ("Greatness and Decline, etc.," vol. iv., pp. 182-83).

[2] "Social progress means the checking of the cosmic process at every step, and the substitution for it of

Huxley, was ever applied by the Romans to the treatment of political and social questions. Even if they had the will, they certainly did not possess the scientific knowledge which would have enabled them to arrest or mitigate the cruel operations of Nature. In ancient times, famine and preventible disease must have swept millions of persons prematurely into the grave.[1] Neither, until of recent years, when

---

another, which may be called the ethical process" (Huxley, "Evolution and Ethics").

The contrast between the public morality of the ancient and the modern world, in so far as the execution of a policy of Imperialism is concerned, is abundantly illustrated, in the case of the Greeks, by the sentence of death passed, at the instance of Cleon, on the whole male population of Mitylene—a sentence which appears to have been rescinded more on grounds of policy than on those of humanity (see the speech of Diodotus, Thuc., iii. 42-45). The main difference between a contemplated crime of this sort—or, to quote another instance, between the crime actually committed by the Lacedæmonians and Thebans in the case of the garrison of Platæa (Thuc., iii. 52-65)—and the crimes of mediæval or even of modern times, such as the Armenian massacres, would seem to be that the former were the deliberate acts of responsible Governments, whereas the latter have more frequently been spontaneous outbursts of savagery, which the responsible Government either could not or would not effectively control.

[1] *The Journal of the Statistical Society*, vol. xli., contains a paper by Mr. Walford on "The Famines of the World,

ANCIENT AND MODERN IMPERIALISM 111

the beneficent Imperialism of modern times has been brought to bear on the subject of preserving human life, was any great improvement effected. The mortality during the great famine in Bengal in 1769 and subsequent years has been variously estimated at from 3,000,000 to "one-third of the population" — that is to say, about 10,000,000.[1] We

---

Past and Present," in which 350 known cases of famine are enumerated. Of these, many occurred in ancient times, and even the scanty records which are extant are sufficient to show the degree of suffering which they caused. For instance, in B.C. 436 there was a famine in Rome. "Thousands threw themselves into the Tiber." In A.D. 42, Judæa was "desolated by famine." In A.D. 278, "thousands were starved" in Scotland. In A.D. 272, "people ate the bark of trees and roots" in England, and so on.

[1] "In the North of Purneah the European supervisor believed that half the ryots were dead; the Resident of Behar calculated the famine mortality at 200,000 in May; the Resident of Murshidabad in June estimated that by that time three-eighths of the population of the province had died; in July, 500 died daily in that town; in Birbhum, "many hundreds of villages are entirely depopulated, and even in the large towns not a fourth of the houses are inhabited." In this large district in 1765 there had been close on 6,000 villages under cultivation; three years after the famine there were little more than 4,500" ("Report of the Indian Famine Commission," 1885, Part III., "Famine Histories," p. 2).

know that in quite recent times the population of the Soudan was reduced, under the inefficiency and barbarities of Dervish rule, from over 8,500,000 to less than 2,000,000.[1] Nowhere does the policy of modern differ more widely from that of ancient Imperialism than in dealing with matters of this sort. The modern Imperialist will not accept the decrees of Nature. He struggles manfully, and at enormous cost,[2] to resist them. In the case of disease he brings science to his aid,[3] and, in the case of famine, his resistance is by no means ineffectual, for he has discovered that Nature will generally produce a sufficiency of food if man can arrange for its timely distribution.

[1] This is Sir Reginald Wingate's estimate ("Egypt," No. 1 of 1907, p. 79), and I see no reason to doubt its approximate accuracy. It is said that 3,451,000 persons died of disease (largely of smallpox) during the few years of Dervish rule, and that 2,203,500 were killed in external or internal—principally internal—war.

[2] For instance, in 1877 some £10,000,000 was spent on famine relief in India.

[3] In the "Transactions of the Epidemiological Society" (vol. iv., Sessions 1884-85), a table is given which shows in a striking manner the reduction of the London death-rate effected since the beginning of the seventeenth century by the introduction of vaccination and other scientific methods.

# ANCIENT AND MODERN IMPERIALISM

The policy of preserving and prolonging human life—even useless human life—is noble. It is the only policy worthy of a civilized nation. But its execution inevitably increases the difficulty of government. In India it has in some provinces produced a highly congested population, and has thus necessarily intensified the struggle for life of the survivors. We have at times heard a good deal of what is called the impoverishment of India. It has been attributed by hostile critics to many causes,[1] with some of which I will not now attempt to deal, as they are foreign to the subject I have in hand. But of this I am well convinced: that whatever impoverishment has taken place is much more due to good than to bad government.[2] It is largely attributable to a beneficent

[1] "Let those who feel for the millions of voiceless cultivators who crowd around relief centres at each recurring famine, or die on the roadside and in obscure villages, bring it home to their minds that famines in India are greatly due to that policy of saddling India with the cost of vast armaments and wars which she should not bear, and which she cannot bear" (Romesh Dutt, "Famines in India," p. xix).

[2] I may quote on this point the evidence of the Rev. Howard Campbell, who worked for twenty years as a missionary in India, and describes himself as a Socialist.

intention to deliver the people of India from war, pestilence, and famine. No such intention ever animated the Imperialists of Ancient Rome, or, in more modern times, the indigenous rulers of Asiatic States.

I have thus dwelt on some of the more salient features which differentiate the task of the modern from that of the ancient Imperialist. To these may be added the fact that Rome was without a rival. The *opes strepitusque Romæ* overshadowed the whole known world. Great Britain, on the other hand, is only one amongst several competing Imperialist Powers, to whom it is conceivable that British dependencies might be drawn by self-interest, partial community of race, or

---

Writing to the *Labour Leader* some few years ago, he said: "I went to India expecting to find a great deal of misgovernment, and most unwilling to admit that any good could result from a bureaucratic system. Experience has forced me to the conclusion that there is no country in the world better governed than India, none in which the administration does more for the masses of the people. . . . The masses are poor, very poor, but their poverty is in no way due to maladministration or misgovernment" ("East India Association Pamphlets,' No. 2).

other causes.  Further, as Guizot has pointed out,[1] the old civilization presented problems for solution of a relatively simple character, whilst those which European civilization has to face are infinitely varied and complex.  If these considerations are borne in mind, there can be no difficulty in understanding why the Romans, in some directions at all events, gained an apparent success which has been denied to their Imperialist successors.[2]

I use the word "apparent" with intention, for, in fact, was the success real?  The answer to that question must depend on the main object

[1] "Quand on regarde aux civilisations qui ont précédé celle de l'Europe moderne, soit en Asie, soit ailleurs, y compris même la civilisation Grecque et Romaine, il est impossible de ne pas être frappé de l'unité qui y regne. Elle paraissent emanées d'un seul fait, d'une seule idée. . . . Il en a été autrement de la civilisation de l'Europe moderne. . . . Toutes formes, tous les principes d'organisation sociale y co-existent, les pouvoirs spirituel et temporel, les éléments théocratique, monarchique, aristocratique, démocratique, toutes les classes, toutes les situations sociales se mêlent, se pressent, il y a des dégrés infinis dans la liberté, la richesse, l'influence" (Guizot, "Histoire de la Civilisation en Europe," pp. 35-37).

[2] It is, I think, capable of proof that economic causes and trade interests greatly facilitated the execution of Roman Imperial policy; but I will not at present attempt to discuss this very interesting question.

which it is held that an Imperialist policy should seek to attain. If, at any period, either during the Republic or the Empire, the question of *Quo vadis* had been propounded to a Roman Imperialist, I do not conceive that he would have found much difficulty in giving an answer. He would have said that he wished, above all things, to maintain his hold over the provinces, either because they were profitable, or because he feared the consequences which might result to the Empire from their abandonment; that he did not particularly wish to interfere with local institutions more than was necessary;[1] that, rather against his will, he had been obliged, in some cases, to extinguish them, as their continued existence had been found, in practice, to clash inconveniently with the necessities of his Imperial policy; and that the liberality of his intentions was strongly

[1] Mommsen ("Hist.," vol. iii., p. 237) says, speaking of the days of the Republic: "The Roman provincial constitution, in substance, only concentrated military power in the hands of the Roman Governor, while administration and jurisdiction were, or at any rate were intended to be, retained by the communities, so that as much of the old political independence as was at all capable of life might be preserved in the form of communal freedom."

## ANCIENT AND MODERN IMPERIALISM 117

exemplified by his treatment of the Greeks, whom he had not endeavoured to Romanize,[1] partly because it would have been extremely difficult to do so, and partly because, although he did not much like this mercurial nation, he nevertheless recognized that the sort of intellectual primacy which they enjoyed rendered it both necessary and justifiable to accord to them some special treatment. But he would have added that the last thing in the world he intended was to put into the heads of the provincials that, by copying Rome and Roman customs, they would acquire a right to sever their connection with the Empire and to govern themselves; in fact, that his central political conception was not to autonomize, but to Romanize, or at least Hellenize, the world.

What answer would the modern Imperialist give to the question of *Quo vadis?* I do not think that the Frenchman, the Russian, the German, or the Italian, if the question were

[1] "Wherever the Greek civilization had taken root, the Roman policy was rather to extend than to supplant it. In the East, the Romans were content to work through the Greek form of civilization, and to act as the successors of Alexander. They did not Romanize; they Hellenized" (Arnold, "Studies, etc.," p. 196).

put to any of them, would be much more seriously embarrassed than the ancient Roman to find an answer. Each would reply that his intention was to civilize his alien subjects, but in no way to relax his hold over them. But what would be the reply of the leading Imperialist of the world—of the Englishman? He would be puzzled to give any definite answer, for he is in truth always striving to attain two ideals, which are apt to be mutually destructive—the ideal of good government, which connotes the continuance of his own supremacy, and the ideal of self-government, which connotes the whole or partial abdication of his supreme position. Moreover, although after rather a dim, slipshod, but characteristically Anglo-Saxon fashion, he is aware that empire must rest on one of two bases—an extensive military occupation or the principle of nationality—he cannot in all cases quite make up his mind which of the two bases he prefers. Nevertheless, as regards Egypt, he will—or at all events, in my opinion, he should—reply without hesitation that he would be very glad to shake off the Imperial burden, but that at present he does not see much prospect of being able to do so. His Indian problem is of much greater complexity, and more especially presents difficulties unknown to the Imperialists, whether of the ancient or the modern world.

Consider what has happened in India. The most practical and energetic of Western has been brought into contact with the most contemplative of Eastern nations, with the result that old ideals have been shattered, and that the very foundations on which the edifice of society rests are in process of being undermined.[1] On what foundation is that edifice to be rebuilt? The idea that haunts the minds of a very few Westerns, and of a larger number of Orientals, that native society, whether in India or in other Eastern countries, can be reconstituted on an improved native

[1] Whilst this essay was passing through the press I chanced to read a very good—because, I believe, very true—account of the present condition of society in India, written by Lady Cox, and published in the November number of the *Nineteenth Century*. It is much more worth reading than most Blue-Books. Lady Cox evidently has a deep sympathy with the natives of India, and, moreover, she combines knowledge of her subject with sympathy, which is not always the case with some of her countrymen who speak and write on Indian affairs.

model, is a pure delusion. The country over which the breath of the West, heavily charged with scientific thought, has once passed, and has, in passing, left an enduring mark, can never be the same as it was before. The new foundations must be of the Western, not of the Eastern, type. As Sir Henry Maine very truly remarks,[1] the British nation in dealing with India "cannot evade the duty of rebuilding upon its own principles that which it unwittingly destroys." The most salient and generally accepted of those principles is unquestionably

[1] Maine, "Village Communities of the East and West," p. 28. I take this opportunity of mentioning that some remarks I made in my work on "Modern Egypt," vol. ii., c. xxxvii., as to the difficulty of reforming Islam, have been a good deal misunderstood, owing, I have no doubt, to the fact that I failed to express them clearly. Without going at length into the subject, I may say that I did not wish it to be inferred that in my opinion the social system adopted in Moslem countries would not be changed, and, still less, that the reform of political institutions in those countries was impossible. On the contrary, I do not in the least doubt that both social changes and political reforms will take place. What I meant was that these changes would almost inevitably produce this result—that the Islamism of the future would probably be something quite different to what we imply when we speak of the Islamism of to-day. To this view I adhere, but what the Islamism of the future will be is a point on which I do not venture to prophesy.

# ANCIENT AND MODERN IMPERIALISM 121

self-government. That must manifestly constitute the corner-stone of the new edifice. There are, however, two methods of applying this principle. One is to aim at eventually creating a wholly independent nation in India; the other is gradually to extend local self-government, but with the fixed determination to maintain the supreme control in the hands of Great Britain. It cannot be doubted that the aspirations of a considerable section amongst the educated classes of India now point in the former of these two directions. Speaking only of those who profess the Hindoo religion, their opinions may differ as to the time which should elapse before those aspirations can be satisfied; but so far as I can judge from recent discussions, the only difference between the extremists and moderates is that, whereas the former wish to precipitate, the latter would prefer to delay, the hour of separation.

If India were a single homogeneous nation, the execution of a policy of this sort might perhaps be conceivable.[1] But it is nothing

[1] I notice in the "Moral and Material Progress Report for 1906-07," p. 161, that one obscure newspaper advo-

of the kind. In the last census[1] no less than 147 distinct languages were recorded as vernacular, and I find on examining the detail that, if account be taken only of the languages spoken by communities of more than a million people, 276 million speak twenty-three different tongues.

If now we turn to the question of diversity of religions, we find that, besides a sprinkling of Parsees, Christians, and Buddhists, there are $62\frac{1}{2}$ million Mohammedans, of whom some, though their creed is that of Mohammed, have adopted Hindoo forms and ceremonials.[2] Two hundred and seven millions are classed as Hindoos, who are split up into an infinite number of sects.[3] To quote the words of the very able compiler of the census: " Within the enormous range of beliefs and practices which are included in the term 'Hinduism' there are comprised two entirely different sets of ideas, or, one may say, two widely different

---

cates the adoption of a "Creed of India," with a view to amalgamating all the diverse Indian races. The idea would appear to be quite incapable of realization.

[1] "Indian Census," p. 248.
[2] *Ibid.*, p. 375.    [3] *Ibid.*, p. 360.

conceptions of the world and of life. At one end, at the lower end, of the series is Animism, an essentially materialistic theory of things, which seeks by means of magic to ward off or to forestall physical disasters, which looks no further than the world of sense, and seeks to make that as tolerable as the conditions will permit. At the other end is Pantheism, combined with the system of transcendental metaphysics."[1]

To speak of self-government for India under conditions such as these is as if we were to advocate self-government for a united Europe. It is as if we were to assume that there was a complete identity of sentiment and interest between the Norwegian and the Greek, between the dwellers on the banks of the Don and those on the banks of the Tagus. The idea is not only absurd; it is not only impracticable. I would go farther, and say that to entertain it would be a crime against civilization, and especially against the voiceless millions in India whose interests are committed to our charge. The case is well put by a very intelligent Frenchman who visited India a few years

[1] "Indian Census," p. 357.

ago. "The question," he says, "is not whether England has a right to keep India, but rather whether she has a right to leave it. To abandon India would in truth lead to the most frightful anarchy. Where is the native Power which would unite Hindoos and Moslems, Rajputs and Marathas, Sikhs and Bengalis, Parsees and Christians, under one sceptre? England has accomplished this miracle."[1]

As a result of the discussions which have recently taken place in connection with Indian affairs, it has been decided—I think, on the whole, wisely, though I entertain some doubts in respect to certain details — to associate natives of India to a greater extent than here-

[1] Paul Boell, "L'Inde et le Problème Indien," p. 289. M. Leroy Beaulieu also says ("La Colonisation," vol. ii., p. 418): "La disparition d'une souveraineté Européenne aux Indes serait un malheur et pour ce pays et pour la civilisation en général." Mr. Rice Holmes, on pp. 141-43 of his "History of the Indian Mutiny," gives a very graphic, and I believe absolutely correct, account of the anarchical state of those portions of India in which, for the time being, the strong arm of British authority was relaxed. I wish the younger generation of Englishmen would read, mark, learn, and inwardly digest the history of the Indian Mutiny; it abounds in lessons and warnings.

tofore with the executive government of the country. It has also been decided to go at one bound to greater lengths than appear to me to be wise in the direction of effecting legislation through the machinery of representative bodies largely composed of elected members. It is now useless to hazard any conjectures as to what consequences will be produced by these bold experiments. We must await the result with what patience we may. But there is one note which was slightly struck in the course of the discussions, and to which it will, perhaps, not be superfluous to allude. Some Englishmen appear to think that our duty lies in the direction of developing self-governing principles all along the line, and that we must accept the consequences of their development, whatever they may be— even, I conceive, to the extent of paving the way for our own withdrawal from the country. I do not say that any Englishman would regard this final conclusion with pleasure, but possibly some would be inclined to accord complacent acquiescence to what they would consider the inevitable. Within reasonable limits, I accept the interpretation of our duty. I do not conceal from myself that the consequences may be serious, in so far that they may materially increase the difficulty of governing the country;[1] but I altogether reject the extreme consequence of possible withdrawal. I deny that such an ultimate result is inevitable — at all events, within any period of which we need at present take account—unless we ourselves weakly acquiesce in the inevitability. Let us approach this subject with the *animus manendi* strong within us. It will be well for England, better for India, and best of all for the cause of progressive civilization in general, if it be clearly understood from the outset that, however liberal may be the concessions which have now been made, and which at any future time may be

[1] The difficulty of reconciling British democratic institutions with the execution of an Imperial policy was fully recognized by Mr. John Bright. Writing to Sir James Graham on April 23, 1858, Mr. Gladstone said: "I have had a very long conversation with Bright this evening on India. . . . He admits the difficulty of governing a people by a people—*i.e.*, India by a pure Parliamentary Government" ("Life and Letters of Sir James Graham," vol. ii., p. 340).

I think that the Duke of Wellington once said, though I am unable at this moment to lay my hand on the reference: "If ever we lose India, it will be Parliament that will lose it for us."

made, we have not the smallest intention of abandoning our Indian possessions, and that it is highly improbable that any such intention will be entertained by our posterity. The foundation-stone of Indian reform must be the steadfast maintenance of British supremacy.

In this respect something of the clearness of political vision and bluntness of expression which characterized the Imperialists of Ancient Rome might, not without advantage, be imparted to our own Imperialist policy. Nations wax and wane. It may be that at some future and far distant time we shall be justified, to use a metaphor of perhaps the greatest of the Latin poets,[1] in handing over the torch of progress and civilization in India to those whom we have ourselves civilized. All that can be said at present is that, until human nature entirely changes, and until racial and religious passions disappear from the face of the earth, the relinquishment of that torch would almost certainly lead to its extinction.

[1] " Augescunt aliæ gentes, aliæ minuuntur,
　　Inque brevi spatio mutantur sæcla animantum,
　　Et quasi cursores vitai lampada tradunt."
　　　　　　(Lucretius, De Rer. Nat., ii. 77-79.)

# APPENDIX

I have endeavoured to ascertain whether, in ancient times, intermarriage was frequent between the dominant races — Greeks or Romans — and the indigenous inhabitants of Asia and Africa with whom they were brought in contact. With a view to the elucidation of this question, I placed myself in communication with others—notably, Sir William Ramsay, Professors Bury and Haverfeld, and Mr. Bevan—of far greater erudition than myself. I am greatly indebted to them for the information with which they have been kind enough to supply me.

It is certain that the marriage of Roman citizens with foreigners was regarded with great disfavour. It was proscribed by law. The offspring of such marriages were considered illegitimate. Virgil condemns the marriage of Antony and Cleopatra in no measured terms.[1] The relations between Julius Cæsar and Cleopatra and other foreign ladies appear to have scandalized Roman society.[2] Titus was reluctantly obliged to part with Queen Berenice, who is said to have been the sister of Agrippa and the wife of Polemon, King of Lycia, and to whom he was greatly attached.[3] So far as can be judged, the feelings evoked in these and similar cases were based solely on national pride and hatred for all barbarians. Perhaps nowhere is the intense dislike which the con-

[1] "Ægyptum viresque Orientis et ultima secum
Bactra vehit; sequiturque, nefas! Ægyptia conjunx."
Æn., viii. 687-88.
Horace calls Cleopatra a "fatale monstrum" (Od., i. 37).

[2] "Dilexit et reginas, inter quas Eunoen Mauram Bogudis uxorem . . . sed maxime Cleopatram" (Suet., Div. Jul., c. 52). Eunoe may have been coloured, but Mr. Sergeant says ("Cleopatra of Egypt," p. 40): "There can be no hesitation in describing Cleopatra as wholly Macedonian-Greek by race." The idea that she had a trace of Semitic blood in her veins does not appear to rest on any evidence of value.

[3] Suet., Div. Tit., c. 7. Gibbon, however, characteristically insinuates ("Decline and Fall," c. liii.) that the reluctance of Titus to part with Berenice was not very real, as at the time of the separation " this Jewish beauty was above fifty years of age."

servative Roman entertained against foreigners and the introduction of foreign customs more clearly brought out than in the remarks which Propertius makes about Cleopatra.[1] She was accused of placing the "barking Anubis" in competition with Jupiter; of having caused the jangling sistrum to be substituted for the Roman war-trumpet; and of having introduced into Rome the terrible innovation of "disgraceful mosquito-curtains."

In spite, however, of prohibitory laws and Roman prejudice, it appears certain that intermarriage between Romans and members of the subject races was no uncommon incident. I have in my address (p. 96) alluded to the evidence adduced by M. Boissier and Sir William Ramsay as regards Numidia and Phrygia. The Roman soldiers who were taken prisoners by the Parthians in B.C. 53

[1] " Ausa Jovi nostro latrantem opponere Anubim,
  Et Tiberim Nili cogere ferre minas;
Romanamque tubam crepitanti pellere sistro,
  Baridos et contis rostra Liburna sequi;
Fœdaque Tarpeio conopia tendere saxo,
  Jura dare et statuas inter et arma Mari."
                                        Prop., iii. 11.
[*Baris* (βάρις) was the Egyptian name for a boat.]

married native wives,[1] and although Horace considered this as a disgrace, he would equally, as Sir William Ramsay writes to me, have " regarded it as disgraceful if they had settled on the Elbe and married German wives, or on the Thames and married British wives, for he couples, two lines earlier, Britons and Parthians together as foes."[2]

I cannot anywhere find any distinct indication that colour antipathy, considered by itself, formed a bar to social intercourse, and therefore to intermarriage. Juvenal, indeed, appears to have regarded the black skin of the Æthiopian as a physical defect, which he classes in the same category as bandy legs.[3] But here, again, it must be remembered that he lashes all foreigners—Greeks, Jews, and Egyptians—indiscriminately with his satire, quite irrespec-

[1] " Milesne Crassi coniuge barbara
  Turpis maritus vixit."
        Hor., Od., iii. 5.

[2] " Præsens divus habebitur
  Augustus adiectis Britannis
  Imperio gravibusque Persis."

[3] " Loripedem rectus derideat Æthiopem albus."
        Sat., ii. 23.

tive of the colour of their skins.[1] When Virgil in his second eclogue, speaking of Menalcas, says, " Quamvis ille niger, quamvis tu candidus esses," he appears to be merely alluding to a matter of personal taste in distinguishing between the rival merits of two suitors belonging to the same race.

Turning to the case of the Greeks, it is to be observed that a decree issued by Pericles forbade the enrolment as citizens of Athens of the children born of foreign marriages. They were, however, considered as legitimate in the private relations of life, and were allowed to inherit family property. The Petrie papyri show that the original Greek settlers in Egypt brought their wives with them (Mahaffy, " Silver Age of the Greek World," p. 45), and this view seems to be confirmed by a chance observation of Diodorus Siculus (xx. 41), in which, speaking of the march of Ophellas' army through Libya, he says that the soldiers were accompanied by their wives and children (πολλοὶ δὲ τούτων τέκνα καὶ γυναῖκας καὶ τὴν ἄλλην παρασκευὴν ἦγον).

[1] See, *inter alia*, Sat., iii. 60, 296; x. 174; xv. 1, 2, 115-123.

## APPENDIX

Gorgo and Praxinoe, who are the principal characters in the well-known Adoniasuzæ of Theocritus, must have accompanied their husbands to Alexandria. They boasted of their Peloponnesian descent, and of their Doric accent :

Συρακοσίαις ἐπιτάσσεις;
ὡς δ᾽ εἰδῇς καὶ τοῦτο, Κορίνθιαι εἰμὲς ἄνωθεν,
ὡς καὶ ὁ Βελλεροφῶν · Πελοποννασιστὶ λαλεῦμες ·
Δωρίσδεν δ᾽ ἔξεστι, δοκῶ, τοῖς Δωριέεσσιν.

A remark made by Polybius (xxxiv. 14), to which Professor Bury has drawn my attention, appears to be conclusive on the point that a mixed race sprang up at Alexandria. Polybius (B.C. 210-128) visited that city, and does not appear to have been at all favourably impressed with its condition. The population, he says, consisted of three distinct classes—viz., first, native Egyptians, " an acute and civilized race " (φύλον ὀξὺ καὶ πολιτικόν); secondly, mercenary soldiers; and, thirdly, "a mixed race, who were originally Greek, and have retained some recollection of Greek principles" (τρίτον δ᾽ ἦν γένος τὸ τῶν Ἀλεξανδρέων. . . . καὶ γάρ, ἐι μιγάδες, Ἕλληνες ὅμως ἀνέκαθεν ἦσαν, καὶ ἐμέμνηντο τοῦ κοινοῦ τῶν Ἑλλήνων ἔθους).

Mr. Bevan refers me on this subject to the information contained in M. Bouché-Leclerq's "Histoire des Lagides" (vol. iv., c. xxviii.), from which it would appear that marriages between Greeks and Egyptians were of common occurrence—at all events, under the later Ptolemies. M. Bouché-Leclerq gives (vol. iv., p. 94) a copy of a marriage contract between a Greek named " Pers, the son of Bi and Essiur," who was " born in Egypt," and " Nechta, the daughter of Penebhehn and Khephet."

On the whole, I think it may be said that the practice of not unfrequent intermarriage between Greeks and native Egyptians in Ptolemaic times is well established.[1]

As regards other portions of the Hellenistic world, the evidence is very scanty. Alexander, as is well known, favoured a policy of fusion. He himself married a daughter of Darius, and also Roxana, the daughter of the Bactrian Oxyartes; moreover, he obliged some of his Generals to marry Persian ladies. It would

[1] In chapter x. of his "Empire of the Ptolemies," Professor Mahaffy deals with the extent to which fusion had taken place between the Greeks and Egyptians up to the time of Ptolemy IX. (Euergetes II.).

appear from a passage in Arrian (vii. 6), to which Professor Bury draws attention, that this policy did not meet with much success.[1]

Turning to a later period, little seems to be known of the race of *Gotho-Græci*, who sprang up in Bithynia (Bury's " History of the Later Roman Empire," vol. ii., p. 34). It cannot be stated with any degree of certainty that these *Græci* were true Hellenes. Some instances may, however, be given of prominent individuals who possibly contracted ethnologically mixed marriages. The first of the three wives of Constantine V. (718-75) was Irene, the daughter of the Khan of the Khazars. The first wife of Constantine VI. (771-97) was Maria of Paphlagonia, who is generally termed an Armenian, from the fact that during her lifetime Paphlagonia was, for administrative purposes, included in the district of Armenia. Further, the Empress Theodora (810-67) was born at Elissa, in Paphlagonia.' But in the case of all these

[1] See also on this subject Bevan's " House of Seleucus," vol. i., p. 31. Professor Mahaffy ("Empire of the Ptolemies," p. 34) says: "Whether the ladies were repudiated, or whether the whole affair was not considered as a huge joke, as soon as Alexander was dead, we cannot tell."

ladies the absence of precise knowledge in respect to their family histories renders it impossible to say whether they were or were not of purely indigenous origin.

All, I think, that can be said on this branch of the question is that the existence of intermarriage in the Hellenistic world, other than Egypt, is not disproved, and that it almost certainly took place, though with what frequency it is impossible to determine. It does not seem likely that Greek pride of race, which was largely intellectual, should have proved a more formidable obstacle to intermarriage than the sense of superiority based on domination in the case of the Romans.

Mere colour antipathy does not appear to have existed amongst the Greeks any more than amongst the Romans. Sir William Ramsay, writing to me on the evidence furnished by Dion Chrysostom, who, as is well known, praised the virtues of the northern barbarians, and who visited Asia Minor and was thus brought in contact with Orientals, says: " In him, Hellenic anti-barbarian pride is very strong, and yet there is not the slightest trace of mere colour prejudice ; it is civilization-prejudice that moves him, and he can admire heartily certain excellencies even in the rudest barbarians."

I should add that both Romans and Greeks frequently intermarried with the Jews. I have already alluded to the case of Titus and Berenice. Poppæa, though born of a noble Roman family, was converted to Judaism, but her conversion did not hinder her marriage, in the first instance, to a Roman knight (Rufus Crispinus), and subsequently to Nero. A bright spot in her otherwise disreputable career is that she exerted her influence in favour of her co-religionists.

As regards intermarriage between Greeks and Jewesses, the testimony of the Bible may be cited : " Then came he (St. Paul) to Derbe and Lystra ; and, behold, a certain disciple was there, named Timotheus, the son of a certain woman, which was a Jewess, and believed ; but his father was a Greek."[1]

Turning to modern times, I may mention that intermarriage between Europeans and Egyptians is of very rare occurrence ; but it will, of course, be borne in mind that difference

[1] Acts xvi. 1

of religion now imposes an obstacle to such marriages, which either did not exist at all or existed to a far less extent in ancient times. A very few cases of such marriages were brought to my notice during my tenure of office in Egypt. They generally led to such unhappy consequences that I endeavoured—and often with success—to prevent them. Where prevention was found impossible, an arrangement was made under which a European woman who contemplated marriage with a Moslem was fully informed, previous to the marriage, of the main features of the Mohammedan law in respect to polygamy, divorce, and the custody of children; these being, as might naturally be supposed, more especially the subjects on which, as experience abundantly proved, serious dissension was most likely to occur.[1]

[1] Intermarriage between a Christian man and a Moslem woman is even more rare than the union of a Christian woman with a Moslem man. A gentleman, who can speak with authority as regards the practice in Asia Minor, writes to me: "The case of a Moslem woman married to a Christian man is not known to me (the only case which occurred within my knowledge resulted in both being lynched)." I only remember to have heard of one such marriage in Egypt. In that case there was no lynching.

There is in Egypt a very numerous Greek colony, composed of every class of society. But the Greeks form no exception to the general rule; intermarriage with Egyptians is no more common with them than it is in the case of any other European community. There may, of course, have been many mixed marriages of this description of which I never heard, but I do not think that this is likely. I only remember one case of Græco-Egyptian marriage being brought to my personal notice, and I have a distinct recollection of that case, because it gave both the Greek diplomatic representative and myself a good deal of trouble. I am informed by a lady who has travelled a great deal in Asia Minor that in that country intermarriage between Greek women and Moslem men, though of very rare occurrence, does occasionally take place.

There is a further question of some interest which is closely allied to that of intermarriage. I am not aware that any competent scholar has ever examined into the question of the stage in the history of the world at which difference of colour—as distinguished from difference of race—acquired the importance which it certainly now possesses as a social and political factor. It is one which would appear to me to merit some attention.

My own researches are far from profound, and it may well be that I am either ignorant of, or have failed to notice, evidence on this subject, familiar to others who are more fully acquainted with classical and mediæval literature than myself. But, as will be seen from the remarks I have already made, so far as those researches go, I have been unable to discover any distinct indication that colour antipathy existed to any marked extent in the ancient world. The dominant Roman and the intellectual Greek thought themselves, without doubt, very superior alike to the savage Gaul or Briton, and to the more civilized Egyptian or Asiatic; but in estimating his sense of superiority, neither appears, so far as I can judge, to have taken much account of whether the skins of the subject or less intellectually advanced races were white, black, or brown. Is it possible that a differentiation between the habits of thought of moderns and ancients may, in some degree, be established on the ground that the former have only enslaved the coloured races, whereas the latter doomed all conquered people indiscriminately to slavery ? Is it, moreover, possible that, in the early stages of Christianity, the fact that the founder and apostles of Christianity were Asiatics may have carried greater political and social weight than was the case when the West, in spite of antagonism of race, had accepted, whereas the East, notwithstanding racial affinity, had rejected, the new religion ? I merely throw these out as indications of points which may perhaps be worthy of consideration. I shall not be at all surprised if, on further examination, it is held that there is nothing in them.

My own conjecture—and it is nothing more than a conjecture—is that antipathy based on differences of colour is a plant of comparatively recent growth. It seems probable that it received a great stimulus from the world-discoveries of the fifteenth century. One of the results of those discoveries was to convince the white Christian that he might, not only with profit, but with strict propriety, enslave the black heathen. Towards the middle of the fifteenth century, slaves were regularly imported from Senegambia and the Guinea

Coast and sold at Lisbon. "There were eminent divines," Lord Acton says,[1] "who thought that the people of hot countries might be enslaved. Henry the Navigator applied to Rome, and Nicholas V. issued Bulls authorizing him and his Portuguese to make war on Moors and pagans, seize their possessions, and reduce them to perpetual slavery, and prohibiting all Christian nations, under eternal penalties, from trespassing on the privilege. He applauded the trade in negroes, and hoped that it would end in their conversion." It is true that negro slavery never took root in Europe, but it lasted until within recent times on the further side of the Atlantic, and the fact that the institution of slavery was closely identified in the eyes of all the world with difference of colour must have helped to bring into prominence the idea of white superiority, and thus to foster a race antipathy which, by a very comprehensible association of ideas, was not altogether confined to those coloured races who were enslaved, but was also in some degree extended to those who, as in the case of the Arabs, far from

[1] "Lectures on Modern History," p. 53.

being themselves subject to enslavement, eventually became the most active agents in the enslavement of others.

Under the influence of a benevolent and, in this instance, very laudable humanitarianism, there has been a great reaction during the last century ; but I cannot help thinking that even now antipathy based on colour is a much more prominent feature in the government and social relations of the world than was the case in ancient times. There would certainly at first sight appear to be some connection between this circumstance and the recrudescence of slavery, which dates from the fifteenth century.

I make these — possibly rather crude — remarks merely with the object of drawing attention to a subject which is of much historical, and perhaps even of some practical, interest, and in the hope that they may lead to the matter being considered by others more competent than myself to deal with it.

# ImTheStory.com

Personalized Classic Books in many genre's

Unique gift for kids, partners, friends, colleagues

Customize:
- Character Names
- Upload your own front/back cover images (optional)
- Inscribe a personal message/dedication on the inside page (optional)

Customize many titles Including
- Alice in Wonderland
- Romeo and Juliet
- The Wizard of Oz
- A Christmas Carol
- Dracula
- Dr. Jekyll & Mr. Hyde
- And more...

Emily's Adventures in Wonderland

Ryan & Julia